"A Dog Collar in the Docks"

Myra / Remember!

For an old friend of many years /

Bob

Better y
Atlantic Subq

S. MAY 96

Front Cover:
Coming ashore after a Seamen's Service
aboard Kaskelot in 1987
(Photo by John Proffit)

For D'rene

and the

Family

First published 1995 by Countyvise Limited, 1 & 3 Grove Road, Rock Ferry, Birkenhead, Wirral, Merseyside L42 3XS.

Copyright © R A Evans

ISBN 0 907768 76 8

Photoset and printed by Birkenhead Press Limited, 1 & 3 Grove Road, Rock Ferry, Birkenhead, Wirral, Merseyside L42 3XS.

Contents

Acknowledgements

Amongst those who contributed to, and supported, the Mersey Mission to Seamen in the publication of this book special thanks are due to the following persons and organisations:

Atlantic Container Line Agencies (U.K.) Ltd
Bahr Behrend and Co. Ltd
Barclays Bank Plc
Bernard Dowd
Coe Metcalf Shipping Limited
Cory Brothers Shipping Ltd
Cory Towage Limited
David and Ann Lowry
Eric and Grace Knowles
Ernest Townsend
Genchem Shipping Limited
Henry Tyrer and Company Limited
Howard Smith Towage and Salvage
Len and Ann Holder
Liverpool Pilots' Association
Liverpool Pilots' Association (Retired Division)
Liverpool Ship Owners' and Port Users' Association
Mersey Docks and Harbour Company
Terry Malone
Yeoward Brothers Limited

The Mersey Mission to Seamen also acknowledges the continuing support for its work by individuals and organisations, in particular Liverpool Sailors' Home Trust, NUMAST, King George's Fund for Sailors, the International Transport Workers' Federation, The Merchant Navy Welfare Board, The Shipwrecked Mariner's Society, etc and the many other individuals and organisations who support welfare work for seamen through the Mersey Mission to Seamen.

Foreword by Len Holder

The prayer is very true when it says "They that go down to the sea in ships: and occupy their business in great waters; these men see the works of the Lord and his wonders in the deep". Seafarers also see and feel the heights and depths of human emotion in the hazards that they face, through separation from their homes and families, and through great happiness in comradeship and in homecomings. They need a special sort of person to share their joys and support them when they have problems or are feeling low. Bob is that special sort of person.

This autobiography of Reverend Canon R A Evans covers the exciting period after 1956, when Bob was in charge as Chaplain Superintendent of the Mersey Mission to Seamen. Liverpool and other ports in the region were going through a period of change from the great days of the liners to the new trades of the present decade. Change always brings problems, challenges and opportunities for the people involved, and the book is very much about people. To carry out his work needed premises, people and resources. Bob managed to find them.

Sick and destitute foreign seamen, often not understanding the English language, have contacted their families and found their way home with Bob's help. Families with husbands or fathers on the other side of the world have gained comfort and practical support when they have had difficulties or disasters. Many young midshipmen and officer trainees received friendly and sensible advice, and sometimes even met their future wives, through the Mersey Mission. Bob has christened seafarers' children, including two of our own. Seafarers' weddings have been arranged and celebrated despite the need to keep ships manned and sailing on schedule. Many seafarers and their relatives have thanked Bob for helping them through the difficult days after bereavement. At official ceremonies, the flag has been shown and the right words have been said. In the parishes around the North West, congregations know about the deeds and needs of the maritime community.

Foreword

In this book, Bob shows us what Christianity is, through his work and through the lives of those who have known him. His generosity and practicality have always been spiced with a generous helping of Welsh wit, which could always defuse an argument or put a smile on a glum face!

Amongst the many people Bob has known and helped, that count him as a life-long friend, I am very fortunate to have been asked to write this Foreword. Ann and I join Bob in wishing the Mersey Mission to Seamen well for the future and on behalf of the maritime community say "Thank you, Bob!" and all the best to Drene, yourself and your family.

L A Holder
Chairman, Mersey Mission to Seamen Committee

Preface

"What did you do, grand-dad?", asked Katy. It was a good question, so I began to write. The pen took over and this book emerged. There appears to be a lot of "I" in it, yet it is the story of so many people ... and so many are not mentioned, for which they might be grateful!

Tony Lane in his excellent book, Grey Dawn Breaking, looks hard at the British seafarer and ends his Introduction with these words,"Little wonder that in the summer of 1983 the officers' union produced a campaigning leaflet with a photograph of a red ensign and superimposed over it the slogan, Take a good look. Soon you might not get the chance." This book echoes that thought, as Liverpool seems to be turning its back on the sea. The whole world has changed.

A good friend, Dorothy Tucker, reminds me that well over thirty years ago she helped me organise the dances when the rave tunes were Midnight in Moscow and Moon River. Padre John Williams, who so successfully succeeded me as Royal Naval Reserve Chaplain, keeps me in touch with Eaglet and so many old friends. Chance encounters mingle the past with the present and have jogged my memories.

My gratitude extends to so many ... the Ladies' Committee of the Mission with Liz Herzog and her tireless workers, the friendships fostered in the Anchorage Club with Captain Ron Morrison and the rest of the "pirates", the Master Mariners with Eric Moss and Ron Baldwin, the Sea Urchins, the Liverpool Nautical Research Society where I was president for some years, and the countless Groups and Societies where the welcome and support was ever happily afforded. Then add the Flying Angels and there will be a thousand names! Leslie Robertson, Dereck Sadler, Don Rawson, Les Gunn ... the Company Secretaries of the Mission during my years ... we owe them a great debt. The Staff, the Committee, the Voluntary helpers, the Students, the Assistant Chaplains ... this list is really endless. These are the people who sustained the Mission through my years and this story is theirs.

My wife, D'rene, read the pages and revived my memory and kept me going. Pat Ball produced the first version, Simon Williams advised and helped with a further print-out and my elder son, Dr Stephen Evans processed the "floppy disc" for the printer. John Emmerson of Countyvise did the rest. Thank you seems inadequate. But it was Captain Len Holder and his wife Ann who proved to be the final catalyst and without their enthusiasm and expertise the book might not have been published.

The sources of the material are legion, most depend upon my memory, but the influence of Harry Milsom and Sea Breezes is like a drum beat in any writing about the sea. The section on the Nova Scotia is reprinted with permission from the July 1965 Reader's Digest (Copyright 1965 The Reader's Digest Association Ltd). Many personal references appear with the permission of the contributors, but I accept all responsibility for the presentation.

The photographs have mainly been collected over the years or borrowed from friends. In particular, the "Bar Light" was given by Lilian Newell, whose husband, Captain Wilfred Newell, had been the Master of the tug that Christmas. The line-drawings for each chapter are merely my doodles as I waited for inspiration.

Many memories bring back pain, often there is laughter and sometimes incredulity, but the writing has been fun.

R.A.E.

1.

In the Beginning

On the wall of the day room at the Maternity Wing in Whiston Hospital on Merseyside, during the period when I was a part-time chaplain, there was displayed a large coloured poster of the inside of the female anatomy, complete with unborn child, and on the top in bold print were the words: "The First Three Minutes of Life are Critical". Some Liverpool wag had written underneath, "The Last Three are a Bit Dodgy Too!"

The only excuse for that story is that, whilst there may be a prayer, attributed to Sir Francis Drake, which contains the sentiment that "... it is not the beginning but the continuing of the same until it be thoroughly finished that yieldeth the true glory", there still remains the problem of where to start in order to continue.

After ten years working in a mining valley, then on to a barren estate alongside the Dowlais Steel Works in Cardiff and finally in Llandaff Cathedral, I felt the need for a change. I almost returned to the Forces as a Chaplain, but in the end, in complete ignorance of seafaring, I joined the Mersey Mission to Seamen as an Assistant Chaplain only to find myself some nine months later as the Chaplain Superintendent. So for nine months before reaching that exalted position with such a splendid title, I had been the oily rag. There is no better training.

No-one could have been more nervous than when I set out to visit my first ship in Liverpool with my dog collar to the fore.

A Dog Collar in the Docks

Collingwood Dock in the shadow of Clarence Power Station was a jumble of last century's debris and war detritus. The Mission van was parked well clear of the railway lines, the pools of oily water, dockside bollards, hawsers and wires and slowly moving dockers. Up the gangway on that first ship I carried an armful of paper-backs. That ensured my welcome aboard. Blood, murder, rape and mystery filled the off duty hours of most seamen, as at sea they could not walk down the road to the pub, mow the lawn or paper the bedroom. Books never failed.

Walking back to my van, I passed a small, scruffy Irish coaster, which I had previously ignored, and was about to repeat the performance.

"And what's wrong with my ship?"

This came from a character in greasy overalls leaning over the back-end. He stopped me in my tracks, but I had the wit to reply.

"I'll pop back to the van for more books and I'll join you in a tick."

The ship was too small to boast a gangway; so inexpertly I clambered over the side from the edge of the dock. There was no-one in sight, so I wandered about until I found the "oily character", in the galley, putting the kettle over a large coal-fired stove. He turned out to be the Captain, Barry Tyrrell. The ship was the Marazel.

Barry was to give me a life-long friendship. We stayed, as a family, at his home in Dublin, but above all he had taught me the basic rule on ship visiting. The dog collar must not discriminate because no ship is too large or too small and all men aboard are equal.

The mess room in the Marazel was so small that you sat shoulder to shoulder. All those little coasters were the same with about as much space as a caravan. The deckhead above was steel with tired cream paint, supporting a maze of electric cables and a totally inadequate bare light bulb. There we sat with chipped china mugs and tea too thick to stir. In the centre of the table, which was covered with oil-cloth, stood a tin of Carnation Milk with candle runs down the side. I was not sure whether to use the tin for the tea or whether it was there as an ash-tray. Later I was introduced to Irish Stew. It is a tremendous concoction, powerful enough to start the engines, from whence it might have originated!

Barry's father, James, was naturally the head of the family firm and was known in the fleet as Da Tyrrel. I just called him Da. There was one occasion when a man went aboard and Da bought an iron from him. This was not unusual as all kinds of goods were peddled around the ships. However, this character was followed aboard by the local C.I.D. Da was deeply upset when he appeared in court and was fined for receiving stolen goods. Our laughter and leg pulling were of no avail.

That Company tried to employ only Arklow lads, as it was Da's home. Every youngster, on his first trip to Liverpool, would arrive at the Mission with a letter to be delivered in person to me. They came like lambs to the slaughter. There was never any message in the envelope, just a five pound note for the Mission. My task was to make the lad welcome and discuss the sins of the flesh without making them too interesting. For all their bluster, the majority were naive country lads, straight from home with no knowledge of the sea or life. As the youngest aboard was elected to be the ship's cook, regardless of skills, I could always discuss loaves and fishes and miracles!

Arklow Shipping Ltd. has survived in good shape to the present days. The population of Arklow is only ten thousand, the links with the sea go a long way back. Six miles inland there were copper mines in the 18th century at Avoca and the quantities of ore had a dramatic effect on the small fishing port. At the outbreak of the First World War, the harbour was home to 79 trading vessels and 150 fishing boats. The present day Company slowly emerged out of the thirty's depression and now has eighteen ships. When I arrived, there were just three vessels, the Valzell (576grt., broken up in 1972 ... 37 years old!), the Murrell (319grt., also to scrap in 1972) and the Marazell (418grt., sold to the Greeks in 1972). I could not have dreamt that such a small concern could have out-lived Companies as large as Blue Funnel. Barry Tyrrell was correct in reminding me that small can be beautiful.

In the beginning, I was unsure that I had the qualifications for the job. I knew that I could read and write and communicate with a strong Welsh accent. Foreigners seemed to accept me as a foreigner and my accent was particularly welcomed on the Indian ships. With people from the sub-continent, I could speak at a reasonable rate of knots and, of course, up half an octave.

Kingston House - Stage one

However, it took a couple of years to communicate with the Scousers of the Mission staff, but I could assume that they took my arm waving and sing-song ravings as approbation. All seemed to go extremely well with no communication whatsoever, which should confound the man-management experts. In their more lucid moments, I thought that I could pick up the phrase, "It's o'right wack, he's Welsh!" There was no way to discover if I was qualified for the job or not!

The Mission staff were to prove an immense support. Leslie Robertson was the Company Secretary, an expert at translating ideas into reality. He carried all the mundane tasks in his stride and, until his premature death some fourteen years later, we were inseparable allies. Much of the work of setting up the orderly administration of the ten-storey hotel, which we completed in double quick time, fell on to the shoulders of Robbie.

The new hotel addition to Kingston House in James Street replaced our Officers' Club, Merchant Navy House, in Canning Street. That Club had done stalwart work during the war with

Kingston House - Stage 2 underway

rooms for forty men. It was run by Kathy Bridger, who sadly was killed in a road accident in South Africa, whilst there on holiday. Kathy was loved and known by thousands of officers. She was a Cape Horner. That is a person who has rounded Cape Horn in a sailing ship. With her tight bun and blue eyes, the young officers had met their match. At the end of my time on the Mersey many a Master would chat nostalgically about the tender loving care behind such a fierce countenance. I thought she was charming!

The Cape Horner Society adopted me as their Chaplain and over many a splendid lunch tales were told, expanded and gilded. The final lunch, some thirty years on, was in the new Albert Dock on the eve of my departure. My last memories of Liverpool are of the loyalty of the staff and the commitment of the Committee and the real story of the Mission is about their work. The future will rest on the shoulders of those who follow on.

2.

GOOD CHEER

The Early Days

The old stories are the best. If you laughed yesterday and its the same story, you should laugh today. It helps to have a bad memory. One character I met boasted that he had no sense of humour - the original rare bird - and I thought his statement was comic and promptly fell about with laughter. To this day, I cannot understand why he was offended.

Here is one of my oldest stories, which I have trotted out at many a dinner, for many a year. Not everyone laughs!

"The top man in the Army, the head serang in the Navy and the highest flier in the Royal Air Force all chanced to die on the same day and, to their immense surprise, they all arrived at the pearly gates together. Being important people, they began to elbow their way past each other. The gates opened and there was Peter. "Hello, boys bach!", he said. Please note the subtle influence of St. David, which I find a bit encouraging. "There's no need to push as no one person is more important than any other up here. Please read the notice board." And there on the heavenly portals was this notice in best gothic print:

HARK YE ALL WHO ENTER HERE,

YE ALL ENTER AS EQUALS.

Signed,

GOD, Captain R.N.

And that thought about self-important people leads me on to recall an encounter with Robert.

Robert was a Blue Funnel Cadet, aged sixteen and a quarter, and he was angry. In the early sixties in Kingston House, the Headquarters of the Mersey Mission to Seamen, before we built the hotel, the far right corner of the third floor ballroom was the Mecca for the Alfred Holt cadets. At least a dozen appeared each evening and I kept an eye on them, whilst they kept an eye on my Flying Angels.

The first dance that I organised was in the March of 1962 and the build up to that beginning of the beginning was frenetic. Like all parsons, I was not entirely new to the game of setting up a social evening. After all, I had been the organiser of many a Parish Dance and Social Evening for the Cathedral Parish of Llandaff at that famous South Wales extravaganza of the light fantastic, the Bindles Ballroom at Cold Knap in Barry. Moreover, I had been the motivating force behind many a Youth Club Saturday Evening Fling and was adept at placing the seventy-eights on the "Black Box", all strict tempo and Victor Sylvester. I was no fool. Here was a parson well trained in keeping an eye on the young men, who slipped out around the corner for swift halves, resulting in upping the decibels at five past ten, when at last there was no need for

When I was young

the girls to dance together. But, this was Liverpool and I had to think big.

A live band was essential. That was not difficult, as the Liverpool Echo advertised columns of performers every night and, on the telephone, I booked the Hignet Quartet for March 18th and the advent of the cruiser, H.M.S. Tiger. This was thinking big! It was to initiate dances at the Mission every week thereafter on Mondays, Wednesdays and Fridays. There was no mistake, the group was actually called the Hignet Quartet! It was an act of faith.

The next problem was girls. How could I obtain eighty young ladies to dance with my sailors? The answer was inspirationally simple.

All that was necessary was to visit twenty up-market parishes and ask each Vicar to provide four young ladies to help with my dances. What could be easier! For three weeks I toured Merseyside and was amazed at the response to my simple request. I am not entirely sure what it was that those clerical gentlemen thought I was about to organise, but I did feel it necessary to indicate to them that, as they were afraid that their girls might get up to you know what, then in no way would I desire their presence. We had some very peculiar conversations. All this took place before the permissive society had been discovered, but with hind-sight I must have tripped over its birth. The outcome of the three weeks "clergy calling" was a grand total of six girls from the Parish where I lived. H.M.S.Tiger was drawing nearer. I was desperate for girls!

I found the "final solution". Tickets were printed in haste and I toured the shipping offices in the centre of Liverpool. If I came across a young lady vaguely under thirty and she had two legs and was not too bald, she received a ticket. It took two days. I was all set for action with the Hignet Quartet and about one hundred and thirty assorted females. H.M.S.Tiger was almost upon us.

That first night was wonderful. The Hignet Quartet proved to be four fifty year old swingers with dinner jackets, bow ties and a steady beat. They started a decade of live bands at the mission and very soon every night of the week we were rocking and rolling and twisting. I had struck gold.

What I had not realised was that around the corner from us, in the basement of an old warehouse in Matthew Street, there was the start of a musical revolution that would turn the world upside down. This was the Cavern, used by the youngest of teen-agers, drinking nothing stronger than coke. John and Paul and Ringo and George created Beatlemania and we loved them. Their voices were raucous, discordant and untrained, but they belted out a good tune with clear diction and a fabulous beat. They topped the charts with "She loves you" and screamed their way in to a Command Performance. We jumped on the band-wagon. I had long admired the Liverpool Police Band, which could play straight up and down music and then burst with expertise into Rock and Roll. Ron Bailey was a member of that band and he ensured that we had four members every night in the Mission for the latest pop, Gay Gordons, Lily the Pink and Congas through the kitchens and up the stairs, until the whole building rattled and the seafarers sailed away and told the world that Liverpool was the place to be. There was no need for bouncers, we had the best music and the seafarers came in their thousands. I loved it.

The girls were naturally called Flying Angels. The Mission flag carries the outline of an angel and the words, "The Mersey Mission to Seamen". The symbolism of the angel comes from the Book of Revelations, chapter 14, verse 6.

"And I saw another angel fly in the midst of heaven, having the everlasting gospel to preach unto them that dwell on the earth, and to every nation, and kindred, and tongue, and people."

Most Mission stations around the world are called Flying Angel Clubs and, aboard ship, I would announce myself as the Flying Angel Chaplain. So it was right to call my hostesses "Flying Angels". After a probationary period, each one was given a Flying Angel badge to wear with pride.

Sisters brought sisters, and they brought their friends. The numbers grew and Margaret became the "mother superior". We never had less than two hundred and fifty on the books and averaged forty each night of the year.

The Chapel of the Good Shepherd

It was no surprise that a number of girls asked that I prepared them for confirmation. Each night at nine, right in the middle of the dance, I rang the Chapel bell. Many of the girls came down the stairs to the short family service and some nights there would be over twenty men. There was never any pressure put upon anyone. One of the Assistant Chaplains, Russell Owen, was to organise a weekly prayer group and we linked in with some of the ordinands at St. Aidan's Theological College in Birkenhead. Most of this activity seemed to grow naturally and it is only today, thirty years on, that it appears to have been extraordinary. Perhaps the secret was that no-one was forced to do anything. All that was asked of my Flying Angels was that they enjoyed themselves. Everything happened because we were having fun.

Each evening at least one hundred seafarers appeared and for them I had only one rule ... you dance! Last week, now over thirty years on, I was at the River Pilots' Annual Christmas Hot Pot, when I was approached by one of the guests with the mystic words: "I don't know whether to thump you or thank you!" It was a strange start for a conversation. He continued.

Rob and Val Manley - a seafaring marriage

"Thirty years ago I was at one of your dances when my Navy ship was in Liverpool. You came across the dance floor, grabbed my arm, dragged me across and said, "This is Celia. Dance with her". I could have murdered you, but it was the girl I married! May I buy you a drink?"

We enjoyed a glass together, although it would have been somewhat cheaper thirty years before.

Eventually, the era of Disco arrived and I knew that things could never be the same again. Of course, we still enjoyed ourselves. Our disk jockeys were the greatest. Elaine with a smile, which won every man's heart and the irrepressible Maurice with his banjo and Liverpool ditties about "statues exceedingly bare". These days I come across some of my girls, pushing prams with grand-children in them, and then we remember Beatlemania, when the whole world loved Liverpool and Toxteth was just a place and no-one felt deprived or second class and the "race relations board" were incomprehensible words.

It was on one of those nights in the Mission that Robert asked to speak to me. He was obviously upset and wanted to talk. He had just joined Blue Funnel and had started the two week induction course before sailing on his first trip to sea. This was the big break from school and home, out into the world. As an officer cadet, he was staying in the Company Hostel at Riversdale, just around the corner from where I lived in South Liverpool, on the edge of the Mersey.

My liaison with the principal of the Hostel, Dick Hutson, was excellent. I had, in fact, already met Robert as I visited the Hostel every Thursday evening to have dinner and a chat. I was always given a table with seven new cadets. For the occasion they had to wear their best blues and they ate their meal at my speed, as we talked. Then we adjourned to the library, where we drank our coffee. As they had no choice but to put up with me, I unashamedly brain washed them about the dangers of the seafaring life, especially booze, women and disease. I told them how to make the best use of oversea Flying Angel Clubs and stressed the importance of writing home. It was all very formal with no nonsense. At the stroke of seven, I released them. They disappeared like greyhounds. Many were to tell me years after that my advice and talk had proved of great value, even though at the time they thought that I had gone over the top. Robert wanted to talk to a chaplain sooner than most of them.

Actually it was the third time that we had met because apart from our meal together, the cadets were also sent to the Mission for another session. Then I always asked permission to write to their parents to say that we had met. This was rarely refused and most parents wrote back to me with gratitude. The main object of the second session was to introduce them to the library in Kingston House.

The Seafarers' Education Service and the College of the Sea were housed on the same floor as my study and the Chapel. Marjorie Mougne ran the library for many years before her untimely death from motor-neuron disease, when she was succeeded by Liz Edwards. These two were well versed in the provision of books needed for nautical studies.

The Training Colleges sent all their men to use the library. Thousands of seafarers took their tickets by renting our text books and chatting up Bill Eustance, an ex-Harrison Line Master, who gave his time voluntarily to assist the young men.

Many further educational studies were provided in any subject and the students came to us to sit their exams after using the postal courses, whilst at sea. Hobbies and competitions were encouraged. Each year the Seafarers' Painting Exhibition went on display in Kingston House. We tended to take all this in the normal day's work, but the educational spin off for the seafarer was immense. Often I invigilated whilst a man sat an "O" level at the Mission and so enhanced his career. With the eventual decline in British Shipping and the depletion of man-power, the library in Kingston House was closed after almost thirty years of caring.

Robert was so distressed that we left the ballroom and went into my study. He was angry. A few days before he had joined Blue Funnel, his father had just walked out of the home, leaving his Mum and his younger sister. The father had moved in with his secretary and she, too, had abandoned her little family. It was a familiar story to me.

"What gets me," he said. "My dad is a Director of Education. That's an important job and what right has he now to direct the young, when he behaves like this!"

He talked on and I listened. There was little that I could say. Even now, after all these decades, I can understand his anger because his elders had let him down badly. I hoped that Robert was to manage his life a little better. I wonder if he has!

THE FIRST TO SAY GOOD MORROW

THE LAST TO SAY GOODBYE

Pilots

When I started my work in Liverpool, there were four pilot vessels, taking station in turns off the Bar Lightship, the Planet, which was anchored some twenty miles from the landing stage at Pier Head The vessels were numbered one to four, Sir Thomas Brocklebank, Edmund Gardiner, Arnet Robinson and William Clarke. They rotated on a four week cycle. It did not take long for me to feel at home in them.

The landing stage was almost one of the wonders of the world. It was half a mile long and as you stood at one end in any kind of weather, it undulated like a snake. On it were shops, toilets, booking offices and waiting rooms. In July 1975 the old stage was replaced by a shorter cellular structure, a symbol of modern technology. Sadly in February 1976, there was a Force Ten gale and the technological wonder sunk. Someone did point out at the time that the old wooden wobbler had been there for a hundred years and had survived all that God and man had thrown at it.

Every Thursday morning one of the pilot boats would tie up at the stage, as the new crew arrived and provisions were loaded. This was when a dozen or so certificated River Pilots and the young apprentices also went aboard. My first trip with them was memorable.

We set off at eleven by the Liver clock. New Brighton with its lovely pier and Perch Rock with its lighthouse were one side, as we sailed down the river, and, on the other side, stretched the miles of Liverpool Docks with the Port Radar Tower at the north end. Then we moved out into the buoyed channel, negotiating a sharp dog-leg to the left with the masts of Paddy Henderson's Pegu, still above water, where she had sunk in wartime. The in-coming ships appeared to aim right at you, but the channel was actually like a dual carriage way and the road was safely marked with buoys, each one numbered and carrying a flashing light.

The water changed colour as we left the murky Mersey to disperse its filth into Liverpool Bay. The coastal line below Southport and, on a good day, the finger of Blackpool Tower were on the right. Then, in the distance the Welsh coast and the Great Orme at Llandudno stood clear, if you knew where to look.

There was rarely less than a dozen ships waiting to come in and another dozen outward bound. My memory went back to 1946, when aboard the Reina del Pacifico, I returned from South Africa and disembarked at Birkenhead. Sixteen years later, here I was aboard number two Pilot Boat, taking up station off the Bar Lightship. I was to get to know that lightship and her seven men crew and the swaying lantern. We had arrived.

Lunch was served and I sat alongside the Master. Was it Captain Stanley or Captain Treganza? I cannot recall. Captain Stanley, like a professional, weaved magic tricks with playing cards and introduced me to whisky and milk to keep me upright. Captain Treganza was brimful with improbable tales to test my gullibility. There at the long mess table sat all the pilots with the Master at the head, sharpening a knife to carve the joint. He knew the cuts for each man as the plates moved down the table. It was like dining with a family and the talk was incessant. This was the way in which the juniors learned their trade, as experiences were shared. The food was excellent. Perhaps I would not have eaten so well, that first time, had I but known what lay ahead.

The vessel remained on station for a week, so the time came for my departure. I had wondered about it. Two decks down, we were at the water's edge and there was the pilot launch. She was extremely small and not much more than a dinghy with a motor at its back-end. The crew comprised a couple of apprentices, who seemed to relish the thought of baptising the Padre by total immersion. The object of the exercise was to convey a pilot across the water to an in-coming ship and, of course, to remove a pilot off any out-going vessel. Twenty miles from the landing stage, the waters tend to go up an down. At that moment it looked to me like the middle of the Atlantic!

Carefully I waited on the small ladder on the side of the pilot vessel and then, as instructed, when the two craft came together, I launched myself into the cutter. I did not enjoy that desperate leap, but was grateful for the steadying hands of my betters.

So we set out to board my first in-coming ship, the Octavia. The size of the cutter quickly became evident, when we left the shelter of the pilot boat and hit the sea amidships, swaying with careless abandon in rhythm to the rise and fall of the waves, which now looked excessively steep. I sat clutching the sides, thinking pious thoughts, which later might have been interpreted as "nearer my God to Thee". And this I was to discover was the easy bit!

We came alongside Octavia. Up went the pilot. Then my case was hauled up. That ship towered above me like a three storey house and down its side hung a rope ladder. I was encouraged to believe that there was no problem, although one apprentice did suggest that I should get it right the first time. It was comparatively simple. I waited until the cutter was on the crest of a wave and then grabbed hold of the ladder. I did just that and then made a discovery, which had not been explained. As soon as I grabbed the ladder, the cutter had disappeared from under me and I was left dangling, like a curate with no visible means of support. So up I went.

At the top were some of the ship's company, as surprised to find a Padre, as I was to see them. They hauled me over the side by the scruff of my neck. It seemed a rather undignified way to meet my flock, but I was much relieved to be there. I stayed aboard some three hours, whilst we went up river, through the lock system and eventually tied up at Langton Dock. I felt that it had been an excellent way to introduce myself to a ship's company and was to repeat the exercise many times after that first perilous run.

Thereafter I often reflected on that opening venture, which must have found much elbow room in my subconscious. It seemed to sum up a valid approach to life. Boarding that ship, in that way, had required a positive decision and, once taken, there was no way to retreat. You could not even stand still on the ladder to work out the next move, because the next wave was coming along. There was only one choice. Having taken the decision to go for it, you had to go up the ladder. Then came the great surprise. I was welcomed aboard. Faces had looked down with smiles and hands stretched out to haul me aboard. My reflections told me that all that was required from me was the first step and then I was accepted by the seafarer.

Over the years I was able to establish very close contact with the Liverpool Pilot Service. Wherever I went I seemed to trip over a river pilot. I think that their Association was to allocate a member to every pub on Merseyside and, in fairness, there was also at least one in every church that I visited. And like the Mersey Mafia, wherever I went, they looked after me

The Liverpool Pilot Service was formed under an Act of Parliament in 1765 and within a decade they had established themselves. There were to be nine pilot boats, all cutters, 36 feet long and displacing forty tons. Each cutter carried seven pilots, three apprentices and a master. Two masters did turn and turn about and the boats were based off Anglesey, Hoylake and, of course, in the Mersey. In 1770, three cutters were wrecked and, of the twenty-eight lives lost, twenty were pilots. By 1773, there were eleven boats, 127 pilots and 32 apprentices. By 1825, there were 140 pilots and in 1860, 199 and 55 apprentices. Steam was introduced in 1896. When I started in 1961, there must have been about 200 pilots. Now thirty years later the same volume of trade is handled by the port as in 1961, but the ships are so large and efficient that today the movement is handled by a mere fifty pilots and they have just taken on the first apprentices for twelve years.

It was a proud moment for me when I was asked to lead a Service of Thanksgiving for the 222 years of the Liverpool Pilot Service to be held in Liverpool Parish Church of Our Lady and St. Nicholas. For all those years the Liverpool Pilot Service had been an independent institution, possibly the oldest in Liverpool, and that all came to an end in October 1988, when all pilots were absorbed into the Mersey Docks and Harbour Company. This was the climax of an era and a sad time for reflection, as so many men were made redundant and the Service trimmed to meet the new needs of the Port.

The Parish Church was packed to the doors. One of the pilots, the short, stocky and bearded John Curry, had written a poem to mark the end of the 222 years.

> We men of the dawn
> Come from seawards
> Learning the river's ways
> We mastered
> Our Business in her waters.

I recalled a vivid passage from a book entitled, "Liverpool by an Old Stager", which captured the mood of bygone years, the salt and smell of the Port and the pride and pain of the people. The book was written in 1852, just four years before the Mission was founded.

"We are at the dock-side, or on the pier head. The tide is rising, the wind is favourable, "The sea, the sea, the open sea", is the word with all. What bustle and confusion! How the men swear! How the dock masters rush about! What "horrible confusion worse

A Dog Collar in the Docks

confounded" seems to prevail! And yet there is method in all this seeming madness. Order will presently come out of all this present chaos. The vessels pass through the dock gates. Meat and bread are tossed aboard of them at the last moment. Friends are bidding farewell! Wives tremble and look pale. There is a tear in the stout-hearted sailor's eye as he waves his adieu. But, "Give way there my lads; heave away my hearties!" The vessel clears the dock, passes through the gut, and then pauses for a brief space at the pier, while the sails are set and trimmed Then comes the final word, "Cast off that rope!", and many a time have we, at hearing it, tugged with our tiny hands until we have succeeded in effecting it, and then strutted away as proudly as if we had just won Waterloo or Trafalgar. And now the sails fill; she moves, she starts, there is a cheer, "Off she goes!", dashing the spray on either side of her as soon as she feels the breeze. And now all the river is alive. The heavy Baltic vessels are creeping away. The Americans, always the same, are cracking along with every stitch of canvas they can carry. The West Indian men sail nobly along like the very rulers of the ocean. There are the coasters, and the Irish traders, and packets, while the smart pilot-boat dashes along under easy sail, here, there and everywhere, almost at the same time. And so they go on until, like a dissolving view, they are lost behind the Rock."

Maybe that was as it really was. Certainly when in the year 1766, when the first Pilotage Act was implemented, fresh in the minds of the founding committee was the fact that just two years previously eighteen vessels had been stranded at the entrance to the Mersey and seventy-five men perished, including some of the pilots at that time. Such was the formal beginning of the Pilot Service.

John Curry reflected upon the past with words from his life.

19

From the bridge
We have seen
Calm seas, prosperous voyages
Tempests, and have heard
Bell buoys tolling in the storm-torn night.

There surely will always be a need for a pilot to direct the vessels into the Mersey, but like the rest of the city and the port, the old order had to change.

Now on the eve
On the flood of every tide
How fares the wind for Liverpool now?
We must set yet another course
There's a new dawn breaking.

I had attended and officiated at many a Service at our beloved St. Nick's, but that Service was special and unique.

So much of my work with the pilots involved the lives of men who had served a lifetime in pilotage and each man could breathe salt air into memories. Naturally I conducted many funerals and as I chatted before each one, I was fed with impossible tales, so that I could embroider the life with fun, courage and absurdity. In the end, I had to accept that the improbable was the truth.

It was expected that, at each departure, I was to use the sailor's version of the Twenty-Third Psalm. There must be many varied interpretations of this much loved psalm. My copy was attributed to J. Woodie Hamilton (U.S. Navy) and was written in 1944.

"The Lord is my Pilot; I shall not drift,
He lighteth me across the dark water,
He steereth me in the deep channels,
He keepeth my log,
He guideth me by the Star of Holiness

for His name's sake;
Yea, though I sail amid the thunder and
tempests of life,
 I shall dread no danger, for Thou art with me.
Thy love and Thy care, they shelter me,
In the Homeland of Eternity
Thou hast anointed the waves with oil
My ship rideth calmly.
Surely sunlight and starlight shall favour me
in the voyage I take
And I will rest
In the port of my God for ever."

Many people have asked for copies of that particular version and I have failed to find any details about the author.

When in my last months in the Mission I was elected to be an Honorary Member of the Liverpool Pilots' Association, I little dreamed that they would afford the further honour of presenting me with a Pilotage Licence of the First Class. I am only the second in the history of the service, which makes me rather proud. At the presentation, I was advised not to let it go to my head and never go near a ship's wheel. They also went to some pains to remind me that a "pilot shall conduct himself with propriety and prudence". Most pilots that I ever met were larger than life in their own lives and the breed continues.

4.

Kabala

A visit today to the South Docks of Liverpool means a shopping spree at the Albert Dock, which attracts over three million folk every year. Granada T.V. Studios, the Modern Tate and the Maritime Museum all vie for your custom.

I still recall our first enthusiasm when the Tate was opened. The fervour was still-born. The first gallery with imposing pillars and brick arcades, where previously tobacco had been bonded, displayed six over-large dreary look-alike, meaningless splodges of modern art. The air was ripe with Liverpool comment. The uniformed attendant did not help with a thunderous stage whisper.

"The artist committed suicide."

There came a very sharp Scouse shaft of wit.

"Was that before or after he painted this rubbish?"

Disgust had overtaken sympathy.

We pressed on in search of enlightenment. But, then we found a table with a broom handle stuck through it, a glass of water on a shelf and a bed made of mouldy sliced bread. I was thankful that I was in mufti, not that Scouse humour pays much attention to the cloth. We came across two children playing havoc with a piece of coiled rope. The mother was doing her best to restrain them.

"Knock it off, lads, that's a bit of art."

The attendant was quick to respond.

"Don't worry, Missus, the cleaner shoves it aside every morning."

By this time we were in a gaggle of viewers and thoroughly enjoyed an afternoon of good humour, cutting sarcasm and incredulity.

We began to think more kindly of our William Brown Art Gallery. After all, "When did you last see your father" does portray real people around a proper table. However, there was one year when I was puzzled by a winner at the annual John Moores Exhibition. It was a large canvas about twelve by four. One half was blue and the other half was yellow! We concluded that the poor chap could only afford two colours.

Never again can I take D'rene to an Art Gallery. Just after I retired, we were on holiday in Cornwall and were invited by the local vicar for afternoon tea, complete with cucumber sandwiches. Unfortunately, as we sat around the drawing room balancing our saucers and plates, it was revealed that one of the guests was a member of the hanging panel at the Tate in London. D'rene went in feet first about dumping their rubbish on Liverpool and graphically described our visit. She was good.

The South Docks for me meant ships. In the sixties, the quaysides were full, even double and triple banking. There were cattle ships from the Isle of Man. They were smelly and small, but I happily sat aboard drinking tea, swapping names and telling the tale. Fruit ships from Spain and the Canaries and grain ships spewing their cargo into the massive silo, filling the air with dust and flurries of feeding pigeons. Small and large, the ships all huddled together on the narrow last century's wharves, amidst the debris of wartime Liverpool. One dock was a jumbled mass of red and rusting lightships and buoys and laid-up floating has-beens. Even the walls of the lock sides were worn into deep grooves by thousands of hawsers, as craft had been warped into their berths. A world of ships had come and gone, each one leaving an unwanted memento of its visit. And it was in my time that the whole scene changed, the ships departed, the muck was moved and all that was replaced by an equally exciting Liverpool.

The South Docks

From my office in Kingston House, I looked down on Salthouse Dock, where sandboats were discharging their cargo with old fashioned grabs into lorries. There across Mann Island I could read fading words on a shed roof, "Sail Making". The red and white flag was always flying from the red brick Pilot House at the water's edge and across the way were the Dock Board Building, the Cunard Building and the Liver Building, all three known throughout the world as marking the Liverpool water-front. It still was the place to be in the sixties.

The southern end of the Liverpool Docks was completely closed in September 1972. The Canning, Salthouse, Albert, Wapping Basin and Duke's Docks were already emptied and ripe for the developer. The Kings, Queens, Coberg, Brunswick, Toxteth, Harrington and Herculaneum ended their usage that September. We were getting very familiar with the phrase "the end of an era".

Apart from the Shipping Federation, from my office I also looked down upon a rather broken down, corrugated iron shed, which boasted the title, "Garden Products". Inside was my old friend, Bob Wink, together with machines producing all kinds of hessian goods. I enjoyed my visits there, although it took me a little while to grasp that the lady in charge of the girls was stone deaf and she could lip read regardless of the noise. There was no need to shout! It was a confusing place.

Alongside that shed an old tank-landing craft, called Landfall, sat on the mud in about two feet of dirty water. It was the home of the Liverpool Master Mariners' Club. I spent many a happy hour aboard Landfall with various clubs and societies, enjoying dinners when into the small hours tales were told, lanterns swung and memories rediscovered of past times over the stilton and the rounds of port and madeira, which circled the table on their silver trolleys. I smoked my beloved pipe with Three Nuns tobacco ... "I'm on number three and she's a mite dry" ... "What about Parson's Pleasure, padre?" ... "Have you tried Presbyterian Mixture?" ... "My wife's condemned me to the shed!" ... "I, too, once tried herbal and the cat left home, but the wife stayed!" No wonder pipe smoking was really a way of life!

The Honorary Secretary of the Mission was Dick Hodges, a Senior Manager of Elder Dempster Shipping Company. He presented a sick communion set for use in the Mission. It had come off the Elder Dempster ship called the Aba and had been used on board during the war. Naturally I was delighted and then did a little research.

Aba was built in 1918 by the Glen Line and was originally called Glenapp. She was one of their first passenger motor-ships. The name was soon changed to Aba when she was transferred to Elder Dempster, who owned Glen Line. Most companies had swallowed other companies as they evolved. Aba carried two hundred and twenty first class passengers and one hundred second class, sailing between Liverpool and West Africa.

The vessel was requisitioned in September 1939 and promptly

sailed to Scapa Flow on the 9th. She was there in time to rescue survivors off the Royal Oak and the Iron Duke.

The famous German submariner, Gunther Prien, in U47 had attacked the Royal Oak, whilst she was at anchor in Scapa in the October. Prien was lost at sea in March 1941.

Aba was involved in April 1941 in the Norwegian Campaign and returned to Liverpool with the wounded and the hospital staff from Harstadt. In May, the German army took Greece and the Aba was the last ship to leave Piraeus in spite of bombing from the air. Next came the battle for Crete and the Aba was caught in Suda Bay and again dive-bombed. On the way back to Alexandria with six hundred and thirty patients aboard and escorted by H.M.S. Coventry, she was heavily bombed for two days and suffered considerable damage.

Aba survived the war to be sold to Bawtry Steamship Company and was renamed, Matrona. Whilst the vessel was being refitted in Bidston Dock in Birkenhead, she suddenly listed and turned over on her side. The Dock Company had her righted, but it was decided to tow her away to be broken up ... a sad end to a remarkable ship. The Aba had had enough! That communion set was a fond reminder and was put to good use.

My contact with Elder Dempster was almost entirely with their West African liner trade, which was a fortnightly service. I looked after the altar equipment on the Aureol, the Accra and the Apapa. The Accra was sold in 1967 and the Apapa in 1968. The Aureol was a beautiful vessel with a white hull and almost yachtlike lines and a well proportioned yellow funnel. She carried two hundred and fifty first class passengers and one hundred cabin class. In 1972, the Aureol left Liverpool to sail from Southampton, but the need for the passenger trade was over and, like so many other ships, she was sold to the Greeks in 1975.

The Elder Dempster ship Kabala tied up in the South Docks. There were about one hundred crew aboard and one of those men I shall not forget.

The story started with a telephone call from the Missions to Seamen Chaplain in Glasgow. He asked that I might visit Kabala, which had just left the Clyde, to meet one of the Nigerian crew, who was being prepared for confirmation.

All Mission Chaplains around the world at that time made use of the same confirmation study course. As each section was completed, the Chaplain would sign the card and this enabled the next Chaplain to continue with the syllabus. As the course was merely an outline, it was easy to adapt it to the needs of each individual seafarer. The spiritual understanding of each person is different and that also includes the Chaplains! My next victim was in the South Docks aboard Kabala.

So I trundled down to the ship, found my man and arranged to see him that night in the Mission. Before I began the lesson, I checked his card. I asked for his full name.

"Fekeregha", he replied. I tried again.

"What's your Christian name?"

"I have no Christian name", he replied. "Why should I? No-one in my home is Christian. They are Mohammedans."

As usual I had presumed too much. We all tend to take too many things for granted. I should have known better.

I remember once helping an Indian seafarer, who had called in for help and advice. His problem was a massive buff form. I have never seen a questionnaire like it. He was applying for British citizenship.

We sat together looking as intelligent as possible. When we reached the section asking for the names, the dates and place of birth of his grand-parents on both sides, he exploded.

"How the hell should I know? Put down that they came out of the trees!"

After confessing that I was equally bemused about my grand-parents and suggesting that mine probably lived in Welsh caves, we both felt better. There was no Somerset House for Indian villages!

In just the same way, Fekeregha came from a different world to ours and I had to make no assumptions. So we chatted about Christian Baptism and for a number of evenings we shared our thoughts. We became real friends and he asked if I would baptise him before he sailed. The date was the 12th June 1961 and the Service took place in the Chapel of the Good Shepherd in Kingston House.

The Service of Baptism, for an adult, is the symbolic washing away of the old life and a positive commitment to become part of the family of God. I still recall standing at the Mission font in our Chapel with some of the Mission staff on one side and some of the ship's company on the other. We both knew the importance of the moment when I turned to him and asked the simple question, "What name do you want?" There must be numerous Dwaines and Debbies and Nickies and Vickies who would welcome the chance to start again.

"Peter".

I had explained that Peter was an excellent name, coming from the Greek word for a rock" and that Jesus had changed Simon's name to Peter, as he wished to build His church on such a rock-like person. We all rejoiced that Peter Fekeregha could be welcomed into the Christian Fellowship.

I never saw Peter Fekeregha again. Such is the life of a Mission padre! Our customers disappeared over the horizon, some would return, but I have always felt that Peter was dead.

The internal Civil War had been raging in Nigeria long before the British press took any notice, although we chaplains were well aware of the genocide. The Muslim Hausas in the North of the country were determined to eradicate the Christian Ibos in the East. The Ibos were being shot on sight and the slaughter was endless. This genocide in modern Biafra was to spread over many years. The world was slow to show any interest and, as there appeared to be no impact on our home economy, our leaders offered no comment.

We had been receiving reports from seamen and from Mission Chaplains that, when a ship arrived in Biafra, the Ibos were taken off their vessel by men with sten guns and then, on the quayside were castrated and shot. I had heard too many stories to discount them. All these horrors passed by unmentioned in our media, but we could not shrug our shoulders. In the Mission, we did all we could to find employment for Ibos in Liverpool. There was no way in which many could return home, as in most cases there were no homes and no families left in Biafra. I more than suspected that Peter Fekeregha was caught up in these killings and so I grew to accept that he was dead. Yet, I felt that Peter would never die!

Since his Baptism in 1961, I was able to recall at least three seafarers, who visited me and they all made the same comment when I asked them why they had approached me to talk about the Christian faith.

"We have sailed with Peter Fekeregha."

That is what I mean when I state that Peter, and folk like him can never die. The names of those three seafarers remain with me ... John, Daniel and Aggrey. Through men like them, we pass on the faith and the flame can never go out for mankind. Peter was no wonder man, no better and no worse than the rest of us, but at least he had learned how to pass on the good to others.

One of my proudest possessions is a ship's bell with its inscription.

"Bob Evans. To mark an arrival and a departure,

Hilbre Island.   15-7-1989"

The departure was, of course, my retirement from the Mission at the end of that month. The arrival was much more important.

On that particular Saturday at the tail end of my ministry in Liverpool, the sky was clear and blue and the wind was strong from the West. Together with my Pilot friend, David Hopkinson, I set out across the sands to walk to Hilbre Island. In my thirty years on Merseyside, this was a wish fulfilled and the whole experience lived up to the magic of that day.

Hilbre Island sits well out on the Western corner of Wirral. It is a natural bird sanctuary and is splendidly isolated from the mainland, when the tide is full. The walk is not clearly defined, but Hoppy, as befits a River Pilot, knew the route as we strode for an hour in our wellies.

The objective was the Canoe Clubhouse. This was a simple wooden structure on the lee of the island, sheltered from the blustery Westerlies. It had been built in the last century. To become a member in those "good old days", you had to paddle your heavy canoe from Birkenhead Docks, down river and across the head of Wirral, to Hilbre Island. I saw photographs of Edwardian ladies, who had achieved this remarkable feat in their long dresses and large hats. One of the original canoes was tucked away under the building.

But, I was there for a special purpose. The reason was a small scrap of humanity, appropriately called Hilbre. My pleasant task was to baptise her.

Hilbre Stafford

It all took place in the open air. The table was a weather-worn carpenter's bench from the last century and there was no need to point out the symbolism of such an altar. The font was an up-turned ship's bell with water which had come from Cape Horn. The Baptism was perfect, with all the wonder of the 1662 Service, and I felt that it was a splendid way to end my ministry to seafarers on Merseyside.

It was a day never to be forgotten and, if Hilbre and those like her, all pass on what they have received, the wonder of what we are about will never die. All that we can do is to leave the world to Peter and John and Daniel and Aggrey and Hilbre and to God.

5.

Just People

Liners meant people. Each passenger liner must have averaged three hundred seafarers and, when I came to Liverpool, the port was host to fourteen such ships. Within a decade they had all departed and their crews with them.

When the Canadian Pacific liner, Empress of Canada (25,284 gross tons), arrived in Gladstone Dock on November 23rd 1972 from Montreal, it really was the end of an era. She was the only trans-Atlantic passenger ship left in Canadian Pacific Shipping. It was also the end of the Liverpool Atlantic passenger trade and the end of the Princes Landing Stage in its old form. Elder Dempster's Aureol (14,083 gross tons) still sailed for West Africa and Aznar Line survived with two ships cruising to the Canaries. But it was not to last.

Coastal services continued with regular Irish sailing by the Belfast Steamship Co. Ltd., and the British and Irish Steam Packet Co. and there was also the much loved link of daily ships to the Isle of Man by the Isle of Man Steam Packet Company.

Canadian Pacific had long indicated change. The Empress of Britain went to the Greeks in 1964, the Empress of England was bought by Shaw Savill Line and the Empress of Canada was sold to Carnival Cruise liners of Miami to be renamed the Mardi Gras and registered in Panama.

Cunard was to be represented in the future by the large Atlantic Container Line's roll-on and roll-off vessels, each with crews of just eighteen. The glory days had been replaced by technology and Royal Seaforth handled most of the trade. For a short while, I was able to care for the Carmania (ex-Saxonia) and the Franconia (ex-Ivernia). Both vessels were 21,000 gross tonnage and had been designed for the Liverpool to St. Lawrence trade, but spent their last ten years cruising. A dispute with the National Union of Seamen over mixing British and Foreign crews ended in deadlock and resulted in both ships laying idle in Southampton and up for sale. That was the end.

I loved to visit the Carmania and the Franconia, even though we knew that the Cunard tradition was changing. Samuel Cunard was born in Halifax, Nova Scotia, in 1787 and the first Cunard vessel to cross the Atlantic was the Unicorn in 1840. Both of the ships that I knew had undergone a two million pound refit in order to cruise the Caribbean in the off season and make the Atlantic in the summer. They were to end their days with the Russians; the Franconia in 1973 was renamed the Fedor Shalyapin and the Carmania in 1974 became the Leonid Sobinov.

When I started in the Mersey in 1961, I visited the Cunard ship called the Media, when she sailed for America with just 145 passengers. When she returned, she was renamed the Flavia and in September 1962, was to operate between Genoa and Sydney. The sister ship, Parthia, was also sold in 1961. At least I had enjoyed a short glimpse of the glory of Cunard.

The previous Franconia was launched in 1922 and was to leave Liverpool on 14th December 1956 to be broken up. That vessel had spent nine years as a trooper and was mainly on the Atlantic run. My connection with the old Franconia is very personal, as the Mission in Liverpool was given the beautiful mahogany chairs from the first class dining room and I sit on number 243 as I type! I wonder how many times my chair has circled the earth!

Because of the liner trade, there had long been the need for centres of excellence and such a place was the Nautical Catering College.

In my early days it was a very tired red brick building in the back streets adjacent to our Cathedral. It was run by a bunch of enthusiasts with Reg Beggs at the helm. The food guaranteed a fairly frequent visit from me and when a new establishment was built in Canning Place, it was even handier for my calls. The new place sported a splendid gymnasium and until I reached the ripe age of fifty, I was able every Thursday morning, before work, to play an exhausting game of badminton with one of my chaplains, Robin Campbell. I never won ... but, the coffee was good.

I first met Malcolm in the Nautical Catering College, just another young lad doing his initial training before he joined one of Canadian Pacific's Empress boats. I did not expect to meet him again because the Liverpool lads had their homes as their bases and had no real need for the Mission in James Street. A telephone call was to alter all that.

The family, that I was asked on the telephone to visit, lived in one of the old terraced houses overlooking the South Docks. The streets were narrow and cobbled and the two-up and two-down homes had brightly coloured front doors, which opened straight into the living rooms. Everybody knew everybody. Generations of families had grown up together to form a caring community. This was the age of the old gas-lit street of yester-year, which was soon to be cleared away to make room for multi-storey blocks.

My task was to break the news of the death at sea of a Maltese cook. To my surprise, it was Malcolm's father who was dead and this I discovered as I talked to the mother and Malcolm's two younger sisters. They were a lovely family and bore the sad news with courage.

There was never an easy way to break news of death at sea. Some just stared and did not believe, others appeared to guess that I had arrived with sad tidings, the majority were numbed and turned to their family for support. All showed great courage.

For a number of years Malcolm's family did well. His career at sea made progress and his two sisters were happy at school. Mother would often pop into the Mission at the end of a shopping expedition and then we would share a pot of tea, chat about her husband as though he was with us, discuss the problems of every day living and, of course, talk about her hopes for her three children.

In time Malcolm decided that he wished to come ashore for work. I can never read the final verse of Acts 27 without the same thought.

"And so it came to pass, that they all escaped safe to land."

My thought had always been that the seafarer's troubles begin the moment he comes ashore and that there he is never safe. Malcolm proved me to be right.

His mother came to me in great distress. Malcolm had been arrested in Manchester. In the court the truth emerged. He had been with two other young men and had broken into a tobacconist's shop to steal cigarettes. The owner lived on the premises, came to investigate, and in the scuffle that followed, he was killed. The charge was murder.

Months of anguish ensued for the little family and I felt helpless in support of them. What can you say in the face of such evil stupidity? I did my utmost to help the mother and the little girls, as the media and the neighbours pressurised them.

Malcolm received a twelve year sentence for murder. I recall the emotions when the verdict was given. The mother did not complain at the findings of the court. She had been in deep shock for so long that the sentence seemed to relieve the tension. She more than accepted that her son had done wrong, desperately wrong, and that he deserved absolute punishment for his crime. At no time did she search for excuses and she made certain that the girls understood that such an action must always be punished. But, the words that I shall never forget came from her deepest feelings as a mother: "He needs my love now more than ever."

They moved from their little terraced house as soon as they could and resettled twelve miles away in the new town of Kirkby. I lost touch as they rebuilt their lives, although every Christmas she appeared for my presents for the girls. Even that stopped eventually.

Sadly, I felt that I had to let them go to find their new way of life.

No-one could have guessed that a tragic event on 14th April 1912 would surface on my desk in the 1970's. The News of the World local reporter was running an article on the sinking of the Titanic and the "failure" of Captain Stanley Lord of the Californian.

Up to that time, Lord was blamed for not coming to the rescue of the Titanic's passengers. Knowing little of the story, my only comment was that I would remember all concerned in my prayers on the Sunday. True to the search for trivia, the News of the World produced this headline, "Chaplain prays for discredited Lord". Although my name was not mentioned in the short article, I assumed that the Bishop of Liverpool did not subscribe to the paper, as I received no communication from him.

A good friend, Harry Milsom, the editor of Sea Breezes was one of the few people allowed to interview Captain Lord, then aged 82.

"The ship seen by the Titanic was moving, so that couldn't have been us because we were stopped. The ship we saw was moving, so that couldn't have been the Titanic, because she was stopped."

The logic of that statement by the Captain of the Californian is very clear. Captain Lord's attempt to clear his name was soon lost in the fury of the First World War. A film, "A Night to Remember", re-opened the accusation against Lord. Captain Lord died in 1961 and the real truth will never be certain.

Communicating with people is never easy. Someone said that , if you are a fool and keep your mouth shut, you will only be thought to be a fool, but if you open your mouth, you confirm it. It happened to me.

For a reason that I cannot remember, I found myself in a pair of shorts refereeing an England versus France (seafaring bunch) rugby match on the Liverpool Police ground. There was trouble before we started, when the French started wittering on about "les substitutes". I really was stupid enough to think that my grasp of that language had cleared the matter.

After half time, I counted the French team and reached the total of seventeen and, as I could not recall the French for fifteen, my solution was to call on two extra Englishmen. Neither side was happy.

Whilst I have a smattering of a number of languages, I was actually a failure in them all, but would never cease to try. There should be an award for effort, even though it was merely a cheery "good morning" and a fluent "how are you?" That was generally enough for the hearer to launch into speech. Each occasion I acknowledged failure, when I heard the words, "Why don't we speak English!"

The greatest interrupter of privacy is the telephone. I was enjoying a morning of study at my desk, as it was my turn to give the weekly Bible discourse the following day, when I received a call from Hull which proved that life in the Mission was not dull. It was a worried mother.

The request was that I visit her daughter in Mulgrave Street in the heart of Toxteth to convey a simple message to her daughter that her husband had docked in Hull and would arrive in Liverpool that afternoon. She stressed that I deliver the news that morning.

Mulgrave Street had seen better days of moderate prosperity in the last century. It is a street of large Victorian houses, three storey, yellow brick and small front gardens. Those gardens were full of refuse, broken prams and beer cans or had been concreted over to park cars of dubious vintage. All the houses needed paint and had been turned into a warren of flats and bed-sits for all the nations of the world.

Like an innocent lamb, I set forth for Mulgrave Street to carry what I thought would be good tidings. I found the flat on the second floor. I gave the door a resounding ecclesiastical knock. A strong African voice greeted me with the Music Hall words, "Who dat out der?" He sounded big. All this faced me with a problem. I had painfully discovered that if I announced myself as "Padre Evans", it elicited the response, "What do you want, Paddy?" It seemed wrong to say that it was "Father Evans", so I took the Anglican compromise and announced, "It's the Vicar!" This was met with an oath and, then, silence.

After a couple of minutes, the door was flung open and there she stood, naked and full frontal. I am not too certain what effect she thought that this display might have on me. My response was safe and simple.

"Good morning, I have a message from your husband."

The effect on her was dramatic. She fled, slammed the door where her friend obviously was, flung on a dressing gown and dragged me into the bathroom.

"What do you mean that you have a message from my husband?"

"Your mother says he's landed today and is on the way home."

"Out!"

I assumed that the "Who dat der" character got the same instruction. I never returned.

At the end of August 1976, the N.A.T.O. Fleet arrived in Liverpool and I was delighted to be asked to lunch by the N.A.T.O. Commodore aboard H.M.S. Norfolk. The Royal Navy does things well, gleaming silver, glasses never neglected, good conversation. On my right was an American Captain, on the left a Norwegian, opposite were Portuguese and Dutch Captains and also the Captain of a German submarine. It was an excellent lunch.

Before leaving H.M.S. Norfolk, we were given the "grand tour" and I was able to examine the Battle Honours of the ship and noted that the previous ship with the name Norfolk had done service in the wartime Russian convoys.

That had been one of the more hazardous jobs of the sea war. When ships were torpedoed in those Northern waters, there was little chance of survival. In 1940, for example, H.M.S. Glorious was sunk off Norway with the loss of 1,474 officers and men, together with 41 men of the Royal Air Force. Only 39 of her complement were rescued. There is no glory in war.

One survivor of the Russian convoys was asked to give his impressions of his experiences.

"Nothing," he replied. "Nothing really."

"But, you must have been bombed, torpedoed, machine-gunned. There must be something you can remember!"

"All that was in a day's work," he responded. The interviewer persisted, "There must be something".

"Yes", he replied at last. "There is something, or rather, two things. I shall never forget the cries of men in the sea at night, when we could not stop to pick them up. The other was the sound of people's voices at home, grumbling in the shops at the lack of goods."

People!

6.

And then there was Christmas

Every seafarer can tell you precisely the number of times in their careers that they were home for Christmas. The reason is too obvious.

When I came to Liverpool in 1961, from my office window on the first floor of Kingston House, I looked across the dual-carriage way upon the entrance to the Shipping Federation, which was run by a national body in London called the General Council of British Shipping, in close association with the Board of Trade. This was really a clearance house, financed by British ship owners, for the placement of seafarers. It was established during the Second World War to provide a pool of seamen to man the British Merchant Navy Fleet. The men simply called it "the pool". Each morning, I could observe scores of unestablished seamen hanging about on the odd chance of getting a berth. This was not easy. One scouser remarked that there ought to be a Union for the Unemployed, so that it would fight the case if they actually got a job! These men were virtually casual labour, attached to no shipping company and only on the fringe of possible employment.

By eleven o'clock in the morning, these characters had crossed the road and were sitting in our ground floor canteen, the Skelton Lounge, where the air was thick with blue smoke and talk. The Skelton Bounty was a local charity and their funds had financed the canteen. When it was furnished in 1957, it was grimly fitted with concrete tables, which were considered necessary for the usage of seamen! I altered all that and made it warm and welcoming. Bertha, short, well built and cheerful, was in charge and controlled everyone with not a moment of difficulty. Most mornings we averaged over one hundred and fifty men there for tea, coffee, OXO, and currant buns or hot buttered toast.

By midday they had all disappeared and most were up the road and safely in the Queens, their favourite pub. Some ventured back to us at three in the afternoon. They invariably failed to negotiate our revolving door at the James Street entrance to Kingston House. A drunk is somewhat surprised to find himself propelled back onto the street, having met no-one in the process!

As Christmas approached, the queue outside the Shipping Federation grew shorter, as men at last were off to sea. The majority of the hard drinkers became teetotal once they were aboard ship and proved themselves to be first class seamen. None of the ship owners wanted their vessels tied up in the docks over the holiday period, which the Liverpool dockers stretched over a full week as they spread Christmas into the New Year. A ship laying idle at the dockside still had to pay dues, so there was a great exodus as the holiday approached. For the same reason many ships stayed out at the Bar Lightship over the holiday to save the cost of being in dock. Few seafarers had the joy of being with their families for Christmas.

Christmas for us in the Mission involved the Bar Lightship. At one time there had been four lightships guarding the Mersey and the estuary. The last remaining was called the Planet and she sat some twenty miles from Pier Head out at the Liverpool Bar.

The first comprehensive chart of the Mersey was produced in 1738 and showed two entrances to the port, the Rock and the Formby Channels. As aids to the seafarers, lighthouses first appeared at Hoylake and Leasowe in the year 1763. The Leasowe Tower still stands today, although it was last used as a light in 1908. In 1771, a light was placed on Bidston Hill and remained there for a hundred years. Many decades were to pass before lights were established at the Point of Ayr, the Calf of Man and the Skerries. Navigation could not have been easy for the seafarer in those days.

A lighthouse, which was built at Formby in 1719, remained operative until 1856 and the structure was not removed until 1941.

The first of the four Liverpool light-ships was built in 1813 and named the Good Intent. She was made of wood, weighed just 78 tons and two Liverpool pilots served as masters. The vessel was sited near the sandbank at Hoylake and, carrying a blue flag, she displayed three white lights in the form of a triangle on her three masts. Twenty years later in 1833, the Good Intent was destroyed on Formby sands during a great storm.

The second Liverpool light-ship, the Milo, was sited off Formby in 1834 and was replaced six years later by the Queen, which was built by Chaloner's of Liverpool.

The third light-ship was at Crosby in 1840, but was replaced two years later by the Prince. This vessel was twice the size of the Milo and the Good Intent and was built by Lairds of Birkenhead. She was the first iron light-ship.

Liverpool was quickly emerging as a major port and in 1873 a fourth vessel was placed at the Bar, which was the entrance to the North-West Channel with its dog-leg passage up the Mersey.

The port developed, battling against nature, as the entry was always difficult because of the shortage of deep water. There was a sand bar about fourteen miles from the dock system over which at low tide there was only eleven feet of water; sand dredging produced the present twenty-five feet. Then limestone was conveyed from the Welsh quarries and twenty miles of embankment were built to form an entry channel. This cleverly guided the flow of the tides to scour the sand and thus ensured the future of the port.

From the formation of the Mission in 1856, the Chaplains always cared for the men who worked on the lightships. Before the Second World War, the Mission launch, the Good Cheer 111, was used by the staff to visit the Bar Light. Good Cheer was sold in 1931. I was intrigued to discover that the first Good Cheer was launched in 1898 and that during that year, after she was blessed by the Bishop, 841 visits were paid to ships on the river, 145 services were held in cabins and forecastles and that 31 of those were in lightships.

When in 1931 the last Good Cheer was sold, the directors of Alexandra Towing Company placed a tender at the disposal of the Mission for the Christmas visit to the Bar lightship. The tender was called the Flying Breeze.

The first tug of that name was built on the Clyde in 1874. She weighed 88 tons and, remarkably, had a screw and rudder at the bows as well as at the stern. This Flying Breeze sank in the docks in 1886, while towing a Johnson liner, and at great expense was raised and put to work again. The saga continued when in 1888 the Flying Breeze and the Flying Whirlwind had a serious collision. Both masters were sacked! Worse was to follow. The Flying Breeze was crushed by the steamer Winkfield in December 1902 and sunk ... a total loss!

The next Flying Breeze was built in 1911 for an amazing £16,315. She was a passenger tender. She was to attend the launch of the Queen Mary and the Queen Elizabeth, but meanwhile saw service in the First World War at Pembroke Dock and at Scapa Flow. At Scapa, where there were some thirty battleships and cruisers, cargo ships and tankers, at anchor, the Breeze acted as a tender, carrying water and stores, ferrying mail and personnel ... and collecting drunks out of the water! Incidentally, the vessel was earning £1,000 each month whilst at Scapa.

During the Second World War, the Flying Breeze was sent to Southampton, but then was quickly returned to Liverpool, where she was busily involved with servicing all the vessels in the convoys. Ninety-one Merchant ships were sunk or badly damaged in the docks by air raids. Out of a total of 144 berths, a third were put out of action. The Flying Breeze survived the lot, but she was not able to outlive the departure of passenger liners from Liverpool; she was the last of the passenger tenders to be withdrawn.

When I went aboard the Flying Breeze just before Christmas in 1961, she was old, very comfortable, but at the end of her life. Sadly thick fog settled on the river. We set out bravely from the landing stage with the hampers for the men on the Bar Lightship, together with the choir boys from St. Gabriel's, Huyton Quarry, but we sailed no further than New Brighton as the fog thickened. The ship carried no radar, so we had to return to the stage and aborting the exercise, we allowed the hampers to go out the next day without us. The choristers drank all the pop and ate all the sandwiches, sang a carol and departed. So ended the love affair between the Flying Breeze and the Mersey Mission to Seamen.

The lightship at the Bar was the Planet. There she sat at anchor with the pilot boat circling and numerous cargo vessels waiting for a pilot to take them into Liverpool after Christmas.

It was a sad day when in November 1972 aboard the Dock Company's Salvor, we towed a Lanby Buoy with its Racon Beacon out to the Bar, unhooked the Planet, and left that automatic contraption to bleep away unaided. It was not much more than a sophisticated unmanned light float with a "what's it" to attract a ship's radar and a non-stop "tooter". Unfortunately, when we stood off to survey this new toy, all was not well, and because the weather took a sudden turn for the worst, a fortnight was to pass before Salvor could come alongside again to rewind the elastic and put an expert aboard to hit it with a hammer.

How sad I felt as the seven men off the Planet walked ashore, carrying their little bags and their memories! It was the end of over one hundred and fifty years of manned lightships in the Mersey. There were no photographers, not a hoot on the river, just our nostalgic sadness. It was like the end of Christmas.

Trinity House looked after all light-houses and lightships around the coast of Britain, apart from the Mersey, and in 1989 the last manned light vessel was withdrawn from service to be replaced with an automatic "thing". This was the Channel Light, about 45 miles north-west of Guernsey, which marked since 1979 the Channel Traffic Separation Scheme. Whilst Liverpool had introduced manned lightships in 1813, Trinity House had placed their first vessel at the Nore in the Thames in 1832. They then provided over fifty around the coasts and today all this is reduced to thirteen automatic light vessels.

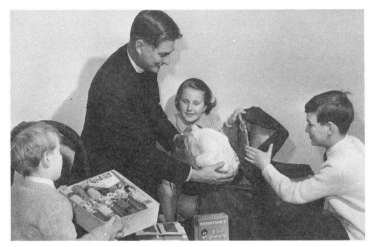

Happy Christmas

Christmas in the Mission really started with the packing of two large, black, oil-skinned hampers with turkey and pudding, crackers and mince pies, every conceivable vegetable and every edible goody. My three children often helped to stuff the hampers as it was a good photograph for the press. Each man on the Planet received a personal present, neatly wrapped and topped with ribbons.

Whilst the departure of Flying Breeze was the end of an era, for the next ten years Alexandra Towing provided a tug ... we had our moments! One year, the weather was bad and our little tug rammed her way out of the river into the channel for the Bar. At each wave, her nose nuzzled into the water which splashed over the bridge, then up she reared to meet the next roller with a resounding smack. This was the life! But unknown to us, the front hatch had been dislodged and the little tug had shipped about five feet of water. The lower cabin was awash. Men moved quickly. It was dangerous. Crammed into the wheel-house was the usual compliment of Granada and B.B.C. television camera crews, all totally unaware of the trauma and merely intent on holding on to their breakfasts. That evening we opened the National News on B.B.C. television at six o'clock with the headline ... "The Day that Father Christmas almost Sank!"

"Over she goes"

In the ten years that we made the journey to the Bar, only three times were we actually able to board Planet, because of the adverse weather. That was when I discovered the immense pride of the men in their work and in their care for the lightship. Every surface shone with polish. They explained their radar screens and communication systems. They kept a constant watch over their parish. No automatic monitor could possibly replace them, but they were to give way to a financial equation and lives would be at risk! I inspected their living quarters and drank scalding coffee. Over the side of the lightship were a motley of fishing lines and I was pleased to return home with chunks of skate and the freshest of fish.

We always took the Bishop of Warrington with us and there was no better companion than Laurie Brown, later to become the Bishop of Birmingham, who smoked a smelly pipe and made us laugh. The hampers were slung across the water on ropes in good nautical fashion and we all lined the side of the tug with cameras turning and the sea heaving. Facing us was the Planet with all her crew assembled. When we were up, they were down. The master of the tug was dressed as Father Christmas and "Ho Ho Ho'd" into a Force Five as we sang "O, Come all ye Faithful". The music came and went as we see-sawed on the waves, the recorders recorded, the T.V. cameras televised and the stomachs rumbled in unison. And there, just the once, swayed the Bishop with his teeth out, parting with his breakfast over the side. One tugman quietly observed: "We brought himself out to raise the tone!"

Then we all tooted our hooters and faced homewards. We left the Planet swinging her farewell with a clang of her bell and a wave of oil-skinned arms. Up the channel we came in good style with marker buoys on either side, all named and numbered, nodding as we passed. Each out-going ship sounded a greeting as all aboard bade sad adieux to Liverpool, outward bound, leaving our little tug with its motley crew and a tree on top of our mast. For those seafarers it was to be yet another Christmas at sea.

So we came home. It always seemed calmer as the whisky bottle appeared by magic and by courtesy of Alexandra Towing. Suddenly we were starving. We munched tomato sandwiches and pork pies and rejoiced at being alive and so intrepid. Christmas is the greatest!

Many times I pieced together an article for the youngest of
the reporters, as they returned from the dead, so that they could
present a copy and tell a tale. All this activity can never again
be repeated off our shores. I suspect that all that we could do
for a Racon Beacon at Christmastide is give it a friendly squirt
of oil ... but only if the weather is kind. Mac of the Liverpool
Echo in one of his headlines spoke for all of us ... "Sick transit
Gloria!"

Christmas Eve was special, when for six years I was the Honorary
part-time Chaplain at the Royal Southern Hospital in Liverpool. It
was the start of a long and happy association with hospitals on
Merseyside. The Southern overlooked the South Docks, so was
extremely handy for popping in at short notice.

Christmas Eve was different. Leaving the dance, which was going
like a bomb in the Mission, I would dash down the road to my
hospital. Nurses and doctors were all assembled. The young trainee
medics could only be impressed by the nurses' cloaks, red sashes
and white head bands, each one carrying a candled lantern which
brightened their eyes and shone their hair. So we toured the wards
with all the lights out, except for our candle light. A nurse or a
doctor read a short lesson, we all sang a carol and I ended with a
prayer and a blessing. Most patients were in tears and Charlie
Dickens would have been proud of us all. Sherry and mince
pies in the canteen, I was rushing back to the Mission.

For me the high light was the Mid-night Service in our Chapel.
The tree, the lights, the candles, the crib, all was ready for us.
Many men would not have received the bread and wine for many a
year. For some, that Service must have been mumbo-jumbo, but
they still wished to share the experience. There were all religions
and liquorice all-sorts of Christians and all were welcome. The
Service was as short and simple as possible with as many carols as
could be squeezed. In the prayers, I tried to remember the countries
and families of each man present. If I missed a country, the man
would speak up and our prayers were a real dialogue with God
invited as a listener. It all seemed so natural. The Lord's Prayer
was said, each man in his own language, and that was right too.

At Christmas you can almost see that God loves each one of us as though there were but one of us to love. You begin to feel like a family. Then, there were more mince pies and sherry and orange juice and much greeting of each other. Everyone talks at Christmas.

So we took the men back to their ships, where in the tradition of their countries, they had their Christmas dinners into the small hours and dreamed of home. There is no more magical word than home. It even beats Christmas!

7.

Padre

Any seafarer of a certain age will talk well about the ships in which they have sailed, the places in which they have docked and, if I chanced to be present, the Flying Angel padres they have met. About most of the padres they would speak in the warmest of tones, often giving the impression that they might even have been related, though not, of course, too closely.

Any story worth telling is worth embroidering. Seafarers are past masters of matching tale with tale in the remembering game. There was one story, which was repeated by the retired seamen so often that it must have had a basis of the truth. I called it "The Legend of Canon Brady", who was the padre at Buenos Aires in the twenties. All seamen just call the place B.A.

The seafarer in a foreign port, and to the foreigner Liverpool was surely that, faced the same problem wherever he chances to come ashore. The dock areas are similar the world over and are very hard on the feet. Communicating with the locals can result in total failure. The city centre is harsh and bewildering. You hold out the money in your palm and it disappears fast as waiters and shop assistants seem to help themselves. The run ashore begins to pall. At last you come to your senses and ask for the Missions to Seamen and in no time you are safe. In most major ports, the seaman makes the Mission his private club. Presents for home, changing money, the right shop to visit, fellow seafarers to chat with, books to read, a good bar with good food and good company, all this is made use of by most seamen, regardless of creed, colour or nationality. In the middle twenties in B.A., Canon Brady offered all this and more.

Brady was known around the world as the Fighting Padre. The centre of activity in his Mission was the boxing ring. He visited the ships and organised the fights for the evening. The men had little money in those days and the Mission was always packed. Apparently Brady would occasionally put on the gloves. The old hands knew that he was lethal and so encouraged the young bloods to have a go at him. The finale was to place all the fighters into the ring together and the last man on his feet was the winner. All those evenings must have ended in pandemonium. How could any seafarer forget Canon Brady? When I spoke to any retired man, it was enough to mention the name Brady.

Towards the end of the last century the Mersey Mission to Seamen produced a man who became a legend. His nick-name was Fell of Frisco and our Chapel in Liverpool has a plaque to commemorate his work as a padre in San Francisco. His was a battle with the crimps.

The crimping system was the norm in this country into the middle of the 1870's. When a ship arrived in port, numbers of men boarded the vessel and "shanghaied" the sailors ashore with the bribe of drink and women. Maggie May of Liverpool would undoubtedly have been one of those ladies. Crammed into boarding houses and full of drink, the men were easily relieved of their wages. In this way, most seamen ended their voyages in the clutches of the crimps, where they remained until they were "sold" back to a ship's master for the next trip.

In the late 1870's the Merchant Navy Act was introduced forbidding the crimps from boarding in-coming ships and also provided seamen with train tickets home and above all a Transmission of Wages Scheme, which enabled back salaries to be paid by Seamen's Money Order. This defeated the crimping system in this country.

San Francisco was another story. Armed with twenty-five

pounds, the Reverend James Fell left the employ of the Mersey Mission and in 1893 set sail for San Francisco. In that port, ninety per cent of the seafarers were British. In three months, Fell had rented a large property for a Mission and set about the crimps. He lodged the seamen at minimum charges and short-circuited the crimps. Stories are told of street chases, but Fell must have been very effective because when he returned home after three years, the crimps had been defeated. When he became a Vicar in the Lake District in 1898, I wonder whether his parishioners realised that he was "a legend in his own time"?

Men like Fell have a remarkable influence on others. The rapid growth of caring for seafarers in America can be traced firmly to the example of Fell. Maybe that happened to me!

In my memory is an Evensong in my childhood church in Llanharan. At sermon time I always snuggled into my mother's coat and dropped off to sleep. There was one evening when I remained wide awake. Padre Wright from the Missions to Seamen in Cardiff was preaching. He was all stories and interesting. One story I have not forgotten.

A small boy was bored and tiresome; so his father went into action. He took a map of the world and cut it into irregular shapes, like a jigsaw.

"Here you are, son. See how long it will take you to put the map together again."

The father assumed that there would be peace for some time, but within five minutes the boy was back.

"Done it, Dad."

This was too much because there was no way in which the child understood a map. He asked how he had done it.

"It was easy", replied the lad. "I have no idea what the map was like, but on the reverse side was a picture of a man. I put the man right, turned it over, and the world was right." I must have been about six at that time and maybe that was just the beginning of the idea of vocation.

There have been many Chaplains, who across the years, have impressed me with sound advice and wisdom. It is not easy to teach the trade of a padre and surely the best way is to learn from each other. Every padre could tell a tale, but none better than David Roberts, the present Missions to Seamen padre in Falmouth. He actually went to sea as a lad in the late twenties and served his apprenticeship on deck in those hard old days. Later, he was ordained and eventually became part of the Missions to Seamen. He was much loved. When David spoke we all listened. There was one of his stories which should not be forgotten. Incidentally, it was told in a Welsh accent!

Radio Officers are lonely people. They are generally employed by the Marconi Company and seconded to a particular ship. The rest of the officers are Company men and belong to each other. Also the trade of radio-man is lonely as he lives apart in his own quarters. They are great people for tapestry and knitting and reading. The padre always made certain that his ship visit included the "radio shack".

David's story was of such a visit to a Radio Officer. In no time, he said, he was sitting chatting happily and asked the inevitable question.

"Is there any particular message which stands out in your mind?"

The officer seemed deep in thought, but after some prompting the words came tumbling out as though a flood gate had been opened. He explained to David that, at a set time each day, Portishead Radio relay messages to all ships at sea. Each ship has its own call sign. On that particular evening the Radio Officer said that his ship was on the list for incoming calls. Eventually the message came through.

"We regret to inform ..."

It was that officer's own mother who had died.

At that point, David recalled, the story stopped, so he gently prodded the Radio Officer to continue.

"We were in the South Atlantic and there was nothing that I

could do. I put the radio system on to automatic, locked everything up and retired into my night cabin."

David told us that by this time he felt that he had intruded into the privacy of the officer's life and wanted to back off, but the story continued.

"I pulled out a sheet of note-paper, sat at my desk and quietly wrote down all the lovely things that I remembered about my mother."

David then looked at me and said that all that he was capable of saying to the Radio Officer was simply, "God bless you."

That tale definitely altered my approach to people. Although I have long concluded that I could not fill a page of note-paper on every person that I meet in life, it can only be that I have not looked hard enough. But, lest I get too sanctimonious, on reflection I am certain that there are some folk whose good points would fit on to a postage stamp!

Its not all cucumber sandwiches and cups of tea being a Mission padre and, in spite of appearances, "beer and skittles" were not on the agenda.

The work of the "Dog Collar on the Docks" could often be misunderstood and condemned. I confess it is generally Christians who condemn! The more liberal characters seemed to think that we were not only on the ball, but often having one! Maybe the two should go together.

I could understand why our life style was open criticism. The fact that Kingston House had three bars would prove too much and they would assume that the place was full of drunks ... and that would include the padre! It was quite untrue. Actually, the old image of the hard drinking seafarer tends to come from the television screen, as no man would keep his job aboard, if he had a serious drink problem. When asked to describe the modern seaman, I would describe him as a "quiet professional", who is also capable of having as uproarious time as the rest of us.

Drink was much more of a problem for the seafarer in my

early days at the Mission and I was glad that we had a working relationship with Alcoholics Anonymous and the Advisory Service.

There was one First Officer, who told me that he had no troubles with booze, but later confessed that he could not go on watch without a drink and he was somewhat surprised when some weeks later his shipping company decided that they could prosper without him. I probed closer and discovered that he always arrived home with a crate of ale whilst on leave. He was convinced that there was nothing wrong in drinking all day when he was home, because he was not on duty. His family was in jeopardy, not that he felt it was his fault. He thought his family was in difficulty because it was a difficult family. He drank at home to avoid the problems of home!

Dismissal from work had brought him to me and I naturally led him to contact A.A. He was to spend a few weeks in the special unit in Deva Hospital at Chester. There he faced his alcoholism for the first time.

For some months he failed to find work and frequently found his way to my study. Eventually, he sailed as Second Mate, a positive drop in salary and status. As his new company sailed between Ireland and U.K., he spent much more time at home. His family became one again and he never returned to his old ways. "Once an alcoholic, always an alcoholic". Years later I chanced to call at his home and I recall a remark he made.

"Now I see the world in colour."

I think I knew what he meant, because if you really look, we are surrounded by glory.

Drink can put a padre at risk. Whenever I was seen at the bar, I invariably had a glass in my hand, but all was not what it seemed. It was known as a Padre's Special. Often I placed my order in a good strong voice, all heads would turn, the customers perked up and took note of the contents. There were many suggestions as to what it should be, but no-one got it right. In fact, it was nine-tenths lemonade with a touch of bitter to colour it. I do not recommend it, yet it kept everyone happy and probably hastened the advent of my false teeth.

When Stuart Blanch arrived as the new Bishop of Liverpool, all his clergy were summoned to the Cathedral. He preached and I actually remember one point he made, even though it was thirty years ago. He told the story of an Olympic Marathon runner, who chanced to be a Christian. Twenty miles into the race the runner "hit the proverbial wall" and was in deep trouble. He resorted to prayer. It was quite simple, like most good prayers.

"Lord, you pick 'em up, and I'll put 'em down."

The point was that when the going is tough, you are never alone.

The Service over, we clergy all lined up in the Western Rooms to meet our new episcopal boss. Dean Patey introduced us. To my surprise, the Dean excelled himself and might have ensured my early departure from the Diocese.

"My Lord, this is Padre Bob Evans. He's licensed by you and by Watneys."

My response was swift and sadly without thought.

"And guess which is the more effective in my job."

The Bishop became a good friend, eventually leaving Liverpool to become the Archbishop of York. But, behind the banter was the fact that as a man relaxed with a drink in his hand, I found many a golden opportunity to be his padre.

There was one evening, when Family Prayers were over in the Chapel and we were on our way back up the stairs to the Lounge Bar and the Ballroom. On the stairs, a German seafarer spoke to me. Actually my Welsh-German is not too bad, but this character was going off like a machine gun and I could barely grasp a word. I thought that I had done well to recognise that he was a German. By chance I had been aboard his ship that afternoon and knew the Second Mate, who was in the bar and spoke excellent English. I dug him out.

"He says that it is a personal matter and will not allow me to interpret."

Here was the language barrier, but I was not defeated.

Down the stairs in my study, I telephoned the German Pastor, Herbert Volker. Along with the Swedish and Norwegian Pastors we used to meet for a Bible study every month, so my contact with Herbert was excellent. I explained the difficulty and the Pastor spoke to the seafarer. We really did have a problem.

The man wished to make his confession. It was Ash Wednesday. He was a Roman Catholic. His ship sailed at eleven that night. It was already 9.45 p.m. and obviously there was no time to take him to the Stella Maris in Hardman Street.

I put a proposition, which the German Pastor communicated to the seaman on the telephone. I suggested that the man made his confession in the Chapel. Obviously I would not understand, but God would. I would then ask for God's blessing upon him for the forgiveness of his sins. The seafarer would not understand, but God would. And, so it was.

We both knelt at the communion rail in the Chapel. He did his bit and, then, making the sign of the Cross, I did mine. At that, we stood up and faced each other. We held our hands to each other. That was a very important moment in our lives.

There we were, two Christians of different brands. Neither of us shared a common language, but we had understood what we had been about. A few years earlier, I had been a R.A.F. pilot and there had been the matter of our two nations at war. Our background, our culture, our ages, everything was at odds. But, for a moment, we were brothers and, in the name of Jesus, we were one. All barriers had been crossed.

Perhaps after all is said and done, there can be the Brotherhood of Man, if only we would give God a chance. Apart from in the Missions to Seamen, where-else could God have effected such a meeting? I was never to meet that man again and I have often wondered whether he remembered that particular Ash Wednesday, as I have done over the passing years. I just pray that he felt as I did and that he has shared those thoughts with his children.

8.

Upside Down and Inside Out

When I became the Chaplain Superintendent, I realised that we all faced the major hurdle of completing the building. All that I had inherited was the four storey block with all the basic amenities for the seamen. The time bomb was the clause in the lease from the City Fathers, who had provided the site with no charge as long as the scheme was completed within fifteen years. No thought had been given to that completion.

The port was busy with well over one hundred ships in at any time. Liverpool was also a centre for training men for the Merchant Navy. They needed accommodation. There was also a need for beds for men in transit awaiting ships and there were those who had no home apart from that provided by the Voluntary Societies. Our only accommodation was our Officers Club in Canning Street overlooking the Cathedral. There we could house some fifty officers, most of whom would be studying for various tickets. It was called Merchant Navy House and had been established in 1941, when the demand was at its greatest.

A visit by Ronnie Swaine, a director of Alfred Holt and the Chairman of the Liverpool Port Welfare Committee, proved to be the necessary catalyst. The Port Welfare Committee with Wilf Patterson as secretary comprised all the voluntary societies on Merseyside concerned with shipping, together with representatives from all sides of the industry, such as Port Health, the Dock Police and Ship Owners. Ronnie asked me a direct question: "Are you going to complete Kingston House?" There was only one possible answer.

We planned a ten storey hotel. There would be sixty-two bedrooms, a dining room with a bar and offices for the staff. The cost was in the region of two hundred thousand pounds. This required an act of faith. We had to believe in what we were about. The year was 1963.

Actually raising large sums of money has never seemed to me to be much more than telling folk about your dream and getting animated. A basic thought is that if the idea is right, the cash will follow. The Mission Treasurer called that "ecclesiastical accounting". Perhaps I should mention that it also requires a certain amount of sweat, blood and tears.

Our Merchant Navy House was sold, grants were obtained from a number of sources, an appeal produced even more cash, bricks were sold at mock auctions by seafarers in the bar, this was getting people animated. Interim payments for the builders, Tysons, were a challenge to the cash flow. That particular Christmas I went on the Bar Lightship "turkey run", knowing that we owed money at the end of the month, which would exceed the bank's loan. I quietly worried. But, when we returned from our voyage, there on my desk was a handsome cheque for the next interim payment. The donor, whom I knew well as I had supped her coffee that week, wished to remain anonymous. She repeated that exercise on two following months ... people are remarkable. In the end the building was completed within the bank overdraft and that was seen off within two years. The venture of faith had been justified.

One unforeseen problem had been the death of the architect, Philip Dod. The difficulty was that the plans had been at the formative stage and most of the ideas had not been committed to paper. In Philip's place came Alan Billinge and he was splendid. Alan was to look after the Mission for many decades.

You would think that after all the heart searching, fund raising and patient planning, the actual day of the opening would be etched deeply in my memory. Truly I cannot recall whether one person did the deed. Obviously the Lord Mayor and the Lord Bishop of

The opening of the Hotel with Donald Crawford and Margaret Hodges

Liverpool would have been present, there would have been a Service of Dedication and naturally there would have been a bun fight. It has all disappeared into the blur of the past. What I have remembered is an encounter with one particular seafarer on that momentous day, but I cannot remember his name!

I assume that the day went well and that I was into the euphoria of peaceful satisfaction. The top brass had long departed and I was in the lounge bar, when a young seafarer came up to me.

"Padre, I've got a complaint."

At first I assumed that I was about to hear another tale, which would end with me recommending a visit to the Seamens' Dispensary, where the "social disease" was hopefully cured. The telephone number of the Dispensary and of the Mission differed by one digit. This led to strange telephone conversations. The caller invariably came straight to the point.

"Have you got my results yet?"

"This is the padre speaking ... try this number."

Thanks were rarely expressed, as the phone was quickly replaced. However, the young man in front of me had a different problem.

It seemed ill-timed, as I was on the crest of my adrenaline and aglow with achievement. I was in no mood for a complaint from anyone, especially this young seafarer.

"Let's sit and tell me what's worrying you."

We sat. He looked very earnest. I braced myself.

"It's the Bible in my room."

That stopped my brain. Obviously I was dealing with a nutter or a non-something or other. He did not look like a Muslim or a Hindu or Russian.

"I don't understand."

In fairness, he hesitated before continuing.

"It's upside down and inside out."

I could think of no intelligent answer, stifled a flippant response and restrained an inane grin.

"Let's go to your room and you can show me the Bible."

He was wrong, of course. I examined the book. It was certainly upside down, but not inside out. It was back to front. The back of the Bible was where the front should have been and conversely ... and the whole thing was probably upside down. The cover had been put on the wrong way and the Bible had been turned ... well!

We relaxed and laughed and returned to the lounge, talking at last like two normal human beings. I had learned something very important about him. He had been the first man in that cabin and obviously had taken the Bible from the bookcase and he had opened it. This told me a little about him, enough to start a serious conversation without any embarrassment. When he left to join his ship a few days later, I had started him on the path of confirmation. I never saw him again, but that Bible is still upside down and back to front and on my bookshelf. I wonder how he is?

For so many people, the Bible may as well be back to front and inside out and I fully understand why they feel that way. How can you blame them! I wonder about Desert Island Discs on the radio, when they say so smugly that the castaway will find a copy of Shakespeare and the Bible. Shakespeare was so ill taught to me in school that I would have been prepared to go to a desert island to escape it and that went for the Bible, which was equally incomprehensible. I certainly needed help and I like to think that I have helped many young men to tackle the Bible with intelligence and understanding.

Music found me in the same state of incomprehension. It was hearing Beethoven's Third Symphony, the Eroica, and Stravinsky's Rite of Spring, being played endlessly on 78's by two music students, Rhys Webber and Tom Lewis, in the room next to mine in College, which eventually forced me to listen and I began to anticipate the sounds like expecting an old friend. These days I love my tapes, but it has taken a lifetime to get there. Maybe that is why we have all been given lifetimes ... to feel at home with Shakespeare, the Bible, our music and the challenge of a desert island.

In the 60's in Liverpool, I used to enjoy a visit to Nile Street where the Chinese seamen had their hostel. The food was great and the welcome was warm. In charge was a Chinese Chaplain, who for some inexplicable reason had been ordained into the Swedish Lutheran Church. It was there that I became aware that a Chinese nod and a smile could actually mean no more than "we hear what you say, but you have no idea of what we think". However, much was revealed when I read in the Daily Mirror that the Chinese Pastor had departed the country in great haste. Apparently, he was from a particularly high caste and had ruled the Chinese staff with severity and, according to the media, with the use of a whip. Maybe that was why their Chapel was always full! The place was closed a few weeks later. I missed the food.

I had no doubt about the integrity of one Chinese seafarer, who had the splendid name of Khong Shen Ping. He was staying with us in Kingston House, taking his Master's "ticket" at the College in Byrom Street. The ticket required a three month's course of intensive study. Unlike most other professions, the seafarer had to pay for his own study time, the course and accommodation. Work, study, sleep was the normal routine. To my delight Khong Shen Ping asked at the start of his time with us that I would prepare him for confirmation. This was a joy for me, because rarely did I have the opportunity to see any man for more than a few days, He was mine for three months.

I was able to throw the book, bookmark and dust cover at him. He responded well and together we learned much about the faith, as we merged our cultures and ideas. Seafarers are not isolated in the bigotry of their own parishes, but have a wide vision of the religions of the world. All this comes not from books as happens to most academics. It is the result of living with other faiths and observing the real impact of a particular creed upon a man. The word "religion" comes from the Latin word "to hold you together". A seafarer is well placed to understand whether a "religion" does just that.

Towards the end of his time with us, I wrote to Bishop Blanch, asking that my candidate be included in the next Confirmation Service to be held in Liverpool Cathedral. I warned the Bishop that my customer was Chinese. In the Service, it was customary for each candidate to hold a card with his name written on it, so that the Bishop might use the Christian name at "the laying on of hands". I felt a warning was necessary, as the word on the card would be "PING".

Ping was duly confirmed on the Saturday afternoon and joined my family for his first Communion on the Sunday in our Chapel. We always had a tremendous breakfast in Kingston House and that day was no different, except that it was also a celebration as Ping had passed his Master's examination. Half way through the meal, he asked a question which stopped the conversation.

"Is it possible to be married next Saturday before I go home to Singapore on the Monday?"

"Of course," I replied, with a mouthful of toast. "Have you anyone in mind!"

Actually, I knew all about his fiancee at home. We all enjoyed the laughter, as we made plans.

"If you can organise your bride at such short notice, I'll organise the church."

The voyage home on the Monday was to be the honeymoon. We set to work.

On the Thursday at Liverpool Airport, we met a charming Chinese young lady, still a little bewildered but armed with two suitcases, one with her bits and pieces and the other, we assumed, held her "instant Chinese wedding kit". When my daughter, Jane, was married, I am certain that it took a month just to find her mother a hat!

The ceremony took place at St. Nick's, our lovely Liverpool Parish Church, commonly called the Seafarers' Church. The Service was conducted by one of my assistant chaplains, Robin Campbell, whilst one of my student helpers, John Blackburn, was the best man. Because of my grey hairs, I gave away the bride. I could never have guessed that, as a Welshman, the first bride that I would give away would be Chinese.

The reception was in one of those mysterious Chinese eating houses off St. George's Square. I found them mysterious because I was never sure of the origin of the species of each offering. There were fifteen courses. The first course was shark's fin soup and the following fourteen were somewhat of a challenge. They all went into the same bowl so every morsel had to be eaten. This made life easy on the washing-up. It was a beautiful meal.

They sailed away and I thought, as usual, that I would never hear from them again. I was wrong. A suitable time later a small card arrived with a happy inscription: "We have a little boy!" And inside were words which ought not to be immortalised. "He's awfully cute from top to bottom and, gee, we're awfully glad we've got him". One can assume that Shakespeare by-passed Singapore. The Card continued. "Weight 6lb 7oz. Length 19 inches. Name ... Derek Khong Heng Chien." This news gave great joy in Liverpool.

My grasp of Chinese is minus nil, but I was intrigued by the names. The Chinese not only have their names back to front with the surname first, Khong, but they actually mean something. The Derek was merely Christian influence; I was concerned about the rest.

The father's name was Khong Shen Ping and the mother was called Irene Sian Sim. Ping means "peace" ... I do not know what "pong" means! Sian Sim translates into "kind heart". So I wrote to them and asked what Heng Chien meant. Back came the answer, "good fortune".

All this was many years ago. In fact, Heng Chien is now twenty. I assume that Ping still works for the Singapore Port Authority. I have not been further East than Aden, but of one thing I am certain, there is one good Christian family in Malaysia. That can be enough to ensure that the faith will be passed on to the next generation and that it will not be "back to front or upside down " and not even "inside out".

9.

Ships and Bottles

When we arrived in Liverpool, our children were aged eight, six and three. Seafarers love tiddlers, which enabled Stephen, Jane and Martin to open many doors for us. In those days, we held a Sunday evening Service at six-fifteen and a number of families attended. It was, of course, good old-fashioned Evensong from the Book of Common Prayer. I loved it, but one evening a group of Greek seamen sat dumbly looking at us, as we sang Magnificat and Nunc Dimittis in Cranmerian English to Anglican chants ... and I felt sorry for them! I decided to change the whole service into modern vernacular, which was exactly what Cranmer had done some four hundred years before. I was certain that Cranmer would have been appalled to discover that we were still using his translations and versions. Thereafter our services were much more informal, much better attended and of deeper spiritual value.

On one occasion, in an old book, I uncovered an early Welsh version of what is now called a Christingle Service and we used it just before Christmas. It was symbolism which the men could understand. At Easter and Harvest, we frequently used slides and snatches of the pop music of the day to help communicate the faith. At least in those days it was possible to understand the lyrics and use them with intelligence.

Perhaps the most colourful attendees on those Sunday evenings were old Captain Johns and his wife, Annie. He was certainly eighty and even though half his tales, which he recalled for the children, were deeply suspect, the other half could have been true and proved to be good listening.

He spoke of smuggling booze for Al Capone, as though he was a personal friend and on the pay roll. The word "prohibition" took on exciting overtones and we did not dare challenge his extravagances. Get him going on the China Seas and the voyage was long and stormy and improbable. We had him repeat his "famous" explanation of how to make a quick buck or dollar or franc with a wave of his stick and a knowing wink of the eye.

"Buy up old rusty chains," he said. "And drag them on the ocean bottom. It's a miracle of nature I'm passing on to you young 'uns, cos they'll emerge bright and as good as new and buy you whisky for the voyage."

This was useless information for any child, but it got the old character into full flow.

Captain Johns had an anecdote and antidote for every subject. Those who sailed with him must have suffered endless monologues with no interruptions allowed. When the news broke that an American had actually walked on the moon, he firmly, in fluent Scouse, refused to accept such ridiculous nonsense, waving his stick in the air and declaring it to be American propaganda against the Ruskies

He was a short stumpy man with a club foot, which meant that he swayed and dipped as he walked; he tackled all forward motion like a runt sized tug battling into a Force Eight gale. I suspect that he kept his teeth in his serge jacket pocket, along with his pipe and tobacco pouch. The pipe "in the pocket" was large and only emerged for use when I was foolish enough to offer him Three Nuns.

"Now would these be Catholics or Protestants?"

His other pipe remained gum-clamped, like Popeye, and as far as I could discern the need for his molars never occurred. Tea was always taken in the saucer. My children were fascinated by him.

One Sunday evening he appeared with a beautifully made ship-in-a-bottle. The sailing vessel carried the name of my elder son, "The Stephen Evans". Whilst not all the secrets were quite revealed, he explained how it was put together. The children hung on every word and then, of course, came the tale.

"It was all a long time ago like, when that bloke Noah was messing about with his Ark and I was the Skipper of a worn out old tub, scratching for cargo off the China coast. Up and down we went for four long years, eating rice and fish, and the next day fish and rice, if you know what I'm getting at. All the crew were Chinkees and with all that rice I was fast going that way meself. That's when I hit the bottle. All day nothing to do except open bottles and empty 'em. It got to a bottle a day."

Typhoons and pirates and yellow plague, all tumbled together. We would be hooked as he sat there, drinking a cup of weak tea with no sugar, blowing into the saucer and pausing for affect and breath. He was just a pale shadow of the man he was describing, but it must all have been true because there was the bottle complete with sailing ship.

"That was when I began to put the ships into the bottles. It would have been a waste to throw the empties over the side"

It was all so logical!

They both lived in Bibby Street, just off the abattoir and St. Ann's Church. The houses were the old back to back construction with no rear entries and only front doors. The first time that I called to visit them was a major happening, as no-one ever passed their threshold. They said that I was the first parson to visit them in all their sixty years together. Annie had suffered a stroke many years before and, whilst she smiled a lot, she never spoke. The Captain sounded off for them both. When he had been at sea, there had been no-one to converse with and safely home, he still felt the need for no contradiction. Maybe he did not notice that Annie never spoke!

My visit produced the best china and a silver teapot. The Captain talked. All was ready. Annie picked up the pot to pour the tea.

We stared at the cup.

"I like weak tea, woman, but this is ridiculous!'

Annie had forgotten to put tea into the pot. It was good for a laugh for the rest of their lives.

Well into their eighties, the couple were moved from Bibby Street to live some three miles further out of town. The City Fathers were planning to demolish the old houses. My two friends were sadly condemned to end their lives in a monster high-rise block. No longer could they travel to Pier Head to smell the sea. Never again did they appear in the Mission Chapel. They were trapped on the eighth floor, afraid to emerge after dark and only able to use the local shops, which barricaded their front windows, even in daytime, in order to prevent vandalism.

"Like bloody Siberia!"

I could not argue with him. It was the end. We gave them a new mattress for the bed and made them as comfortable as possible, but with their old neighbours scattered and the complete loss of security, life was over for them both. They were to die within a few weeks of each other.

Today in Albert Dock in the Maritime Museum, up on the third floor, you will find a real character. His name is Des Newton, complete with beard, twinkling eyes and nautical serge. School groups from Merseyside sit at his feet, as with humorous patter and sleight of hand he demonstrates the art of putting a ship into a bottle. Just before I retired, Des happily presented me with a bottle.

My bottle is different as it contains, not a ship, but a Cross. Des explained. Apparently, early in the last century, seafarers began to put crosses into bottles. At the completion of a voyage, the man would have his bottle blessed by his Parish priest and then it was given a place of honour in the home. There it sat on the mantelpiece, as a thanksgiving for the safe home-coming and survival from the perils of the sea.

The Cross has a ladder leaning against it ... a Jacob's ladder? I never did discover whether this was a reference to Jacob's vision of a ladder connecting earth and heaven (Genesis 28), or whether it stood for the ladder up the side of a ship. I felt that it had nothing to do with Jacob, but was the ladder used by Joseph of Arimathea to remove Christ from the Cross. However, Des insisted that it was the Jacob's ladder. The Cross in my bottle is studded with coloured stones and I shall keep it to mark the end of "my voyage" as Mission Chaplain on Merseyside and as a treasured memento of a friendship.

The nearest that I ever got to Egypt in wartime was a day at anchor off Port Said, before we entered the waterway for a memorable passage down the Suez Canal. What I really recalled was the intense heat, as we lived in the bowels of the troop-ship, and the everlasting plates of Irish stew. Two hair cuts in one day helped with the heat and ample buckets of fresh lime juice kept thirst and scurvy at bay.

The endless Middle East conflicts in the seventies ended with the Canal blocked and numerous ships, including British, were trapped. Every three months or so the trapped crews were relieved and many of them spent the night with us before going home on leave. They all sported their blockade ties as though they belonged to a special club. In fact, they did become a family.

My first long sea voyage from Greenock via the Suez Canal to Durban was aboard the Reina del Pacifico and lasted over six weeks. Troop ships , like the Reina del Pacifico, carried over five thousand troops, all herded together, sleeping in hammocks and nothing to do but sit and think. I was lucky to discover a bridge school and played morning, noon and night with the same partner. We proved a formidable team!

The Reina del Pacifico, owned by Pacific Steam Navigation Company, was launched in 1930 and sailed from Liverpool. The Company offices were just across the road from us in James Street. On her maiden voyage, the ship did the round trip to South America in sixty days, instead of the usual seventy eight. This meant an extra voyage a year! She was 18,000 tons gross and was capable of eighteen knots, carrying eight hundred passengers in great comfort.

During the war she had a charmed life. She helped to evacuate our troops from Norway. There the Luftwaffe attacked the ship off Narvick and a 1,000 lb bomb dislocated communication between the bridge and the engine room. Then she was converted into an assault ship! The task was to place seven thousand soldiers and their equipment ashore at Oran in North Africa and later do the same at Sicily.

I was aboard at the end of 1943. In peace time the vessel carried 280 first class, 162 second and 446 third. I have no idea what class we were. For eight years she was a trooper, sailed 350,000 miles and carried over 150,000 troops. On the 8th July, 1957, she ran aground on Devil's Flat between the Bermuda Narrows and Grassy Bay. On the 11th, two tugs pulled her off and as there was no apparent damage, the four hundred passengers completed the voyage. On the next trip, there was generator trouble and she stopped at Milford Haven. That voyage was abandoned. In November of the same year, she dropped the starboard propeller in Havana and, after being dry docked in Bilbao, she reached Liverpool. The proud vessel was sold for scrap on April 28th 1958 after twenty seven hard years of sailing.

Many years later, in 1993, I was chatting to the Mayor of Kirkby after taking the Royal Naval Association's annual service at St. Chad's and into the conversation at the bar emerged the fact that he had been a cook aboard the Reina del Pacifico. I confessed that I had sailed in her and we established that he was aboard at the same time, but I lacked the courage, or over the years had learned enough tact, and did not tell him that the food had been deplorable and should have been fed to the sharks. We drank our drinks and allowed enchantment and distant view to work their usual magic. We parted as nostalgic friends

In Liverpool I met many an Egyptian crew and the only time that my feet were kissed was when an Egyptian seaman on the verge of a nervous breakdown arrived in my study. He was obviously terrified. Calming him was no easy matter, as I tried to understand his tumbling words. Eventually, I realised that he was claiming that the ship's mate and the crew were planning to kill him. He had appealed to the Master, but had failed to convince him. I was his last resort and he begged for asylum. Unsure as to what I was promising, I agreed to visit the ship and asked him to remain in the Mission. Then he fell on his knees and kissed my feet.

Aboard the vessel, I met a sympathetic Master, who described the problems they had endured from a man who was clearly under great strain. I suggested that a medical officer should settle the matter, as the man was terrified. Eventually after a short stay in hospital, this Egyptian was repatriated. Terror is for real, whether it is physical or in the mind. I wondered what he returned to in Egypt and whether his fear went with him.

Of all the Egyptian ships which came up the Mersey, the one to remember was the Abou Simbel. The crew used the Mission well, coming in great numbers every night. They were a happy bunch and we all enjoyed them, even though some of their cassette music, which they brought with them to play at the dances, might have been alright for a sand shuffle, but was not up to the Mersey beat.

When the ship was due to sail, I decided on a farewell visit. Down in the engine-room, I shook hands with a little finger, as we shouted out best wishes and then popped into the galley with its large pots of bubbling stew and Eastern aromas, through the smoke and chatter of the mess-rooms, I at last arrived in the Master's cabin. No-one was quite as cadaverous of countenance or as friendly as my good friend, Captain Hemida. After an effusive hug and rasp of both cheeks, he placed a cup of Egyptian coffee in front of me. I reckon that you have never lived until you have tasted the Eastern aroma of the Banks of the Nile and are lucky to survive the first sip! The best part of that cup of coffee was the miniscule cup and the only advice that I can impart is important. Drink the top half with caution, leave the rest of the sludge and do not be over profuse in appreciation, lest the cup be refilled. Egyptians love it!

"I have a farewell present for you, padre."

"That is very gracious of you, Captain."

That was a mistake. He poured more coffee. However, I loved receiving gifts as reminders of happy times and smiling friendships. His gift was particularly useless ... a copy of the Koran in Arabic. This is another book which starts at the back and ends in the front!

On the front cover ... that's our back ... the Captain had written something unintelligible in Arabic, which I never had the courage to have translated. Then he added these words: "To my Padre. I respect him. Captain Hemida." This was a tribute which I accepted with the utmost courtesy, but not to be out-faced, I too gave a gift. It was my book ... a copy of the New English New Testament, suitably inscribed, though not in Welsh. It had been an honourable exchange of scriptures.

As a final gesture of goodwill, Captain Hemida escorted me to the gangway and, as we stood there, he pointed to the foremast.

"Do you see that small bundle of oil-skin?"

It was not easy to spot so high on the mast.

"We keep a copy of the Koran up there to remind us that it is our guide and our light."

I could not help but be impressed. Over the years, I had discovered that there was much to learn from other faiths, not necessarily from their books, but from the way in which the men interpret their religion in their lives. That is the true test. Religion is life and there is a prayer which says just that.

> "Lord, what I say with my lips,
> May I believe in my heart;
> And what I believe in my heart,
> May I live in my life."

Meeting men of all faiths taught me that we belong together as one family, the family of God.

The Abou Simbel sailed in the small hours of that night, but something must have gone terribly wrong with the steering and she was almost involved in a collision. The next day I was on the docks again and called to see Captain Hemida, who over coffee told me his tale of woe. I could not resist a crack at him.

"So much, Captain, for your guide and your light!"

With a twinkle in his eye, he was quick to respond.

"No, no, no, it must be this book which you put aboard."

We both grinned at each other. More string was attached and elastic tightened and later that day they sailed.

I was never convinced that the Egyptians paid much respect to machinery. If a radiator fell off the bulkhead on to the deck, it stayed there, because it might have been the wish of Him above. My wife to this day suspects that there might be Egyptian blood in me!

There is great joy when a ship returns. Many weeks later, the Abou Simbel was back with us. I have never forgotten my conversation with my cadaverous friend. He came straight to the point.

"I have read St. Mark's Gospel right through from beginning to end and I love the sound of your Jesus."

It was a grand opening remark.

My advice to all who showed interest was that they read St. Mark. Captain Hemida had read that Gospel like a novel. It is a good story. Most of us read our Gospels odd verses at a time. If we treated an Agatha Christie mystery like that, we would never discover who had done it or who had been done!

I have read St. Mark many times straight through, in one session, in the Chapel. It takes just over two hours. My reaction has always been at the end, "No wonder this man turned the world upside down". In fact I was not surprised that it had worked with Captain Hemida and that he had liked the Jesus that he had met in the reading.

In the same way, I have reflected on Captain John's ship-in-a-bottle. Many people hold on to a faith, as though it should never be questioned or put to the test. They seemed surprised, when I confessed that I questioned my faith and asked questions of myself. But, a faith cannot be kept bottled up safely to be brought out when required. If your faith is to be of any worth, it must be like a ship, prepared to voyage and to face all the storms that lurk over the horizon.

10.

Are you alright, Mac?

Before coming to Liverpool and the Mersey Mission to Seamen, I was on the staff of Llandaff Cathedral in Cardiff at a most exciting time in its fourteen hundred years of history. During the war, the building had been excessively damaged by a German land-mine. My arrival at the Cathedral on All Fools' Day in 1957 was well timed, as the rebuilding had been almost completed.

The most controversial addition was a concrete archway over the Chancel steps carrying a tub-like airborne pulpitum ... that is the Latin for a platform, from which we derive the word, pulpit. This particular pulpitum was designed to hold, not a parson, but a section of the organ pipes. The archway proved to be a natural stage setting for confirmations, ordinations and even orchestral concerts and long before parish churches discovered wandering fonts and movable altars and mobile pulpits, we in Llandaff were making good use of this central position. Gilded angels, which had been rescued from the old bombed organ, surrounded the pulpitum, but the main feature was a controversial figure of Christ in Majesty, which became known as Epstein's Majestas.

That April in 1957, I had sat in the back of the nave to watch the Majestas being placed on the pulpitum and alongside me was the great man Jacob Epstein. He wanted to talk and we chatted for about an hour. With the arrogance of youth, I heard myself asking an impertinent question, but it had arisen out of our conversation.

"How can you as a Jew produce a Christ for a Christian Cathedral?"

We must have been at ease with each other, because after a pause he replied.

"All my life I have been searching for beauty and truth and I find the answer in my idea of the Christ."

Little did I realise that this thoughtful reply would prove to be a link with Liverpool a decade later.

The link was a seafarer called Martin. He was the most gentle of characters, soft spoken with a Wicklow brogue, well dressed and clean shaven, but a drunk. He survived on a diet of rum with all the cunning of an alcoholic, yet he had a natural charm. His sea-going days were sadly over and with no place to live and, I suspected, a diagnosed cancer, I was happy for him to stay with us at the Mission in order to sort out his future. I never did discover where his money came from as every week he received a large cheque through the post for us to cash and then we gave him a daily allowance. He would not talk about it, but I felt that his family had bought him off, in order to keep him at a distance. The result was that he was drinking himself into oblivion and death, abandoned by the sea and his family.

Sadly, like all drunks, Martin very quickly became a nuisance to the other residents and many a night I was called to sort him out. There we would find Martin wandering the Hotel corridors, totally drunk and like a lost soul endlessly asking the same question at the top of his voice.

"Is Christ the King? Is Christ the King?"

Sometimes it sounded more of a statement than a question. I believed that Martin, as a young man, was destined for the priesthood, in true Irish tradition, at the demand of his family. However, he had rebelled and had chosen to be a seafarer. All those years later, he still carried the guilt of failure and all that he was left with was his question.

"Is Christ the King?"

It was a question for all of us.

One day Martin left the Mission and we never saw him again. All that we have to remember him is his drum-beat of a question.

Then another summer came and we seemed to inherit a tramp, who arrived most mornings with some carrier bags full of his belongings. He sat on the wooden seat outside the Mission. That seat was well used, presented to us by a gentleman called Harry Osbourne, who had worked with Rea Towing Company in Albion House on the other side of James Street. It had been made with loving hands in the Birkenhead workshop of the Towing Company and carried a plaque with the words, "For the not so young".

The Mission staff quickly adopted this tramp and gave him a cup of tea each day and then urged him gently on his way. He was no trouble. I felt that we were one of his mansions on his journey through life. I often spoke to him, but there was never any response. Yet, each time before he departed, he scribbled a message on a piece of paper and asked that it be given to the padre. It was always the same, a jumble of unintelligible numbers and words. They made no sense to me, although they could have been mathematical formulas. Perhaps, I should have kept them.

The problem was partially solved, when I received a telephone call from a lady inquiring whether I had met her husband. He was, of course, my tramp. That summer she visited many times with little parcels for me to give to him. I do not know whether they actually met each other. Apparently he was a University lecturer, who had suffered a mental breakdown and had opted out of normal life. Probably he never spoke, because he had nothing to say to me and he showed no concern in what I tried to say to him. By the end of that summer, the seat was empty and we never saw him again. Maybe he had gone back home because his wife made no further contact. Sadly I suspect that he had departed because he had taken as much of us as he could tolerate.

And then there was Bill. He really was a vicious drunk, who would snarl like an animal. Bill drank meths and stank as only man can. No-one could handle him and he spent much time in Walton Prison, "drunk and disorderly". I never understood why such men were ever sent to prison for odd days at a time. He was dirty. I did try to clean him. He would refuse a shower. I offered clean clothes. My poor sinuses were a blessing, when I disposed of his old clobber. Then I felt in need of a bath. In those days I smoked a pipe and that was a great asset.

Bill slept rough every night, yet was never ill. Dirt and meths must keep all known bugs away, except the ones with legs! Having been a seafarer, Bill haunted the docks with the result that it was not unusual to receive an early morning call from the Port Police.

"There's a character here been sleeping it off in the urinals and claims that you know him. Do you want us to book him?"

We all knew that it was Bill and my answer never varied.

"Let him go and he'll find his way to the Mission."

He would not ever go to sea again, as he had set fire to his last ship!

One morning the manager of the head office of Barclay's Bank put in call.

"There's an objectionable drunk, who has spent the night in our entrance and he will not move. He claims that you are a friend!"

"Leave him to me. I'll be there in five minutes."

That was when D'rene bought him socks as his had disappeared in the night. Looking out for Bill was a Forth Bridge job.

Yet there were times when he would arrive at the Mission beautifully dressed and completely sober. I did not discover how he achieved this transformation. In his hand would be a box of chocolates for Muriel, my secretary, who cared in a remarkable way for such folk. She was tremendous. Then Bill would spot me and I knew the greeting. It never varied.

"I don't like you, padre, but I love your lady wife."

I felt that there were occasions when Bill got it right! And, then, as with all these characters, time passed and we realised that Bill had not appeared. We would never know whether he was dead or had just shaken the dust off his feet and abandoned us.

A helping hand is not always appreciated and many a Samaritan earns a black eye for his trouble. Christmas Eve in a city is not a good time. At lunchtime, the offices closed and too much festive spirit would produce the inevitable. The staff at the reception desk phoned through to my study.

"There's a gentleman in the gutter outside the Mission."

"Leave him to us."

The first mistake was to have answered the phone, the second was to suggest that we would do something and the third was not to "pass by on the other side".

We rose to the challenge. With one of my Assistant Chaplains, Russell Owen, I went to the rescue of this character, who in biblical fashion had fallen by the wayside. He was drunk. A large circle of expert advisers had gathered, full of ale and platitudes. No-one knew him. Happily I found an address in his wallet. So we took him home in the Mission van. The Good Samaritan would have been proud of us!

We must have been a brave sight and many lace curtains twitched as the three of us staggered up the garden path. The guy in the middle was by this time in full song ... Ee-I-Adio we won the cup! I could have murdered him. Two parsons and a drunk, weaving together in full view of the sober citizens of Knotty Ash.

The front door opened and there she stood. She was not really a large lady at first sight. The singing stopped. All three of us felt "guilty as charged", not helped by the loving husband, who choose that moment to wish his beloved a "Happy Christmas, my little blossom!"

"What have you been doing to my husband!"

We dropped him and fled. I wonder what the New Testament would have made of that tale?

It was a rare event when an American ship came into Liverpool and those I visited made little impression on my way of life.

The men never wished to use the Mission, regarding us as needed by the poorer nations ... they were right! The seafarers aboard the ships did not seem to have time to stop and talk and I always felt that I was intruding. The welcome was cold. Of course, they had a basic problem. If you wanted a coffee, you used a paper cup in a machine, which did not encourage any social graces. Even cigarettes were not offered, as each person smoked his own. However, there is always the exception. It was an American warship and I have not forgotten the experience.

The surprise was a telephone call from Geoff, the Naval Liaison Officer in Liverpool, requesting that I conduct a Protestant Service for the visiting American warship. I readily agreed that I would report at the required gangway at the precise time. So, armed with my case full of ecclesiastical bits and pieces, I went up the gangway on the appointed dot.

"Who are you, Mac?"

Such was the greeting from a character with his cap tilted almost on his nose and his hands buried in his reefer jacket, which sported three rows of medals. I explained the reason for my presence and words were spoken into a hand set. Another man appeared.

"Follow me, Mac."

I began to get the idea, picked up my case and set out in pursuit.

I had been told that four hymns had been arranged and that they presumed they would fit into my schedule. As we worked our way, into the bowels of the ship, the tannoy spoke.

"Now hear this. There will be a Protestant Church Service in the Mess on Flat Four in precisely five minutes."

As soon as my cassock and surplice were on, I was popped up on a dais, handed a leaflet and abandoned. The Mess was packed with matelots and a great crowd they were. The Service went with much enthusiasm and we all sang with gusto. It was really remarkable.

At the end, I returned to the cabin to remove my clerical clobber and, as I packed my case, my American guide was back. You can guess the next line.

"Follow me, Mac!"

And so I departed.

That evening I telephoned Father Boardman, my Roman Catholic opposite number at Atlantic House, to discover how he had fared with his Service aboard and he started with the old American greeting.

"Are you alright. Mac?"

It became the custom to address each other in this way.

In due time I did receive a charming letter from the American Captain, via our Naval Liaison Officer, in which he expressed an appreciation of my efforts. The complete contrast was a visit to one of the large or small Royal Navy warships in answer to a request for Holy Communion. But, that would be an invidious comparison, especially as it invariably included breakfast with the Captain and the best silver!

Over the years, a number of cadet training ships arrived and we were always involved, It was Russell Thomas, our Welfare Officer, who organised numerous coach trips, as far as York, the Lakes and North Wales. There was always football and it was essential to leave time for shopping. Penny Lane and the Beatles Museum were ever popular. This made Russell a very favoured member of the staff.

On most occasions I was invited to meet the cadets formally for a Padre's Hour. Clan Line were particularly keen and each ship carried a full-time Training Officer. My visit coincided with a parents' afternoon, which enabled me to meet them also. I suspect that it was an excellent public relations exercise to have a padre on tap. What I really enjoyed were the scrumptious cream cakes and the mysterious Indian titbits.

There was one Brazilian ship, when in the Padre's Hour which I handled purely as a "question time", I was asked to explain how a Constitutional Monarchy works! If I had revealed that we also considered the Queen to be the Head of the Church of England, I suspect that they would have demanded that I left as an impostor.

There was one Indian ship, called the Jala Joti, on which I had many good friends. The Captain used to visit our home and on one occasion arrived with an old bridge coat, which D'rene promptly was asked to reline! As a result of this, I might have guessed that there would be a special welcome, when my presence was requested for a Padre's Hour with the cadets.

Naturally, I always expected the young men to be dressed in their best rig, but when I arrived I was startled to find, not only cadets, but all the officers assembled in full uniform. Captain Kamara formally with flourishing arms and flowery words introduced me and then turned with a broad friendly smile.

"There we are then all together. You have one hour to talk to us, padre and we shall be all ears."

He sat in the front row with arms folded. That proved a long hour. At the end, he leapt to his feet.

"There now," he said. "Did I not tell you that he was a great man!"

I dread to think what would have happened, if D'rene had mended his cuffs, widened his trousers and sewed the odd button or two on his shirts.

A Peruvian ship did a first class exercise in public relations on the folk of Liverpool. They had mounted an excellent display of Aztec artefacts and hundreds of people went aboard to visit. The cadets were under the control of a lecturer from the Nautical College in Lima and we organised a full programme for them. The happiest evening for us was having some of the cadets in our home. We fed them and allowed them to walk all over the house and ask questions of the family. Then they sat on the floor and entertained us with guitars and Peruvian Folk music. I hope that they also recall that time with warmth.

The real value of such ship visits was the opportunity for young men to meet as many people as possible and I think we achieved that.

Whilst men in groups will talk well on any subject, the mood changed when I was alone with a man. It enabled him to chat about his family and himself. It almost seemed natural for a man to ask that I said a prayer for his family. The sea is a lonely place to travel. In the same way, when a seafarer came to the Mission, he was not looking for organised religion in any form, yet I was always happily surprised at the numbers of men who would spend a quiet few minutes in the Chapel.

I quickly learned not to underestimate the spirituality of any person, nor to think that nothing happened, even when I assumed that a chance meeting had been fruitless. People need people.

11.

Kirkdale

Whilst my work amongst seafarers in the Port of Liverpool was to be my paramount concern and my first love for three decades, I also found myself involved in parishes. Most Sundays I was out and about preaching in different churches and telling the tale about the "dog collar in the docks". I was never short of anecdotes and most congregations seemed to welcome a breath of salt air. However, there was to be one parish in 1963, which received my full attention. It was called Kirkdale, neatly tucked in between Everton Brow, Scotland Road and the Dock Road.

Kirkdale in the early sixties was coming to the end of its life as a village. The demolition gangs were at work to complete what Hitler failed to do. However, I could catch glimpses of the past.

The little streets of two-up and two-down dwellings fell gently from Stanley Road to the Banks of the Mersey, where they were lost amongst the towering, majestic Victorian warehouses, all symbolising trade and stability. The smell of tobacco, vegetable oils and animal feed filled the mind with oceans of travel and a century of world trade. Cobbles and horses, gaslights and ragged urchins still haunted the memories of the back-lanes and alleys. Kirkdale was not to give up its past easily.

A letter arrived from the Bishop of Liverpool, Dr. Clifford Martin, asking me to be responsible for the interregnum in the Parish of St. Athanasius in Kirkdale. My good friend, Norman Barrow, was moving to taste the delights of All Souls in Springwood. I looked forward to enjoying myself. I was not to be disappointed.

An interregnum is the equivalent of being an honorary grandfather. You are allowed to enjoy yourself, but are not expected to take any decisions, alter any ecclesiastical customs or rock any boats. The amount of time that I could afford was limited by the Mission's activities, but I felt that I could keep the place alive until the next victim arrived to become Vicar.

There were two excellent Readers and two very friendly and competent Church Wardens. It would be good to get the feel of a parish again, if only for a short time. In the event, that interregnum was to last almost a year, but it left me with a smile on my face.

The good people of Kirkdale seemed pleased to see me and said so in their barely comprehensible Scouse accents. The greetings done, they carried on as though I did not exist. This seemed to be very sensible and established a sound working basis.

"If you want anything, just ask."

"What have you got in mind?"

"You know, if anyone's ill or something."

"Don't worry about that."

The parson was expected to take funerals, as and when required. They did their own sick visiting. The cries for help were to be few, as all they really required was a celebrant for their Communion Services. No-one did die as far as I knew. There were to be no weddings. Baptisms were regular with no questions asked. One couple arrived out of the blue for a baptism. I could not turn them away.

"Name this child."

"Francis John Lennon Baker."

"I thought it was a girl."

"It is."

"It's a boy's name."

"There weren't any girl Beatles."

That was irrefutable.

"So it will be Frances with an "e" then", I replied using my intelligence and regretting the lack of interview.

"That's right. We call her Franky."

Some battles are not meant to be fought.

St. Athanasius was a new church building, which let in water every time it rained. Buckets had well established positions. Eventually it was to fit into the environment, but in my time it stuck out like a pre-fab amongst the Victorian surroundings. New wine sits sadly in old bottles.

My first celebration of Communion in St. Athanasius literally left its mark on me. In my travels around the Diocese on behalf of the Mission, I had grown accustomed to varying shades of churchmanship and local peculiarities and the more subtle shades of tradition. It was a minefield for the unwary.

Any itinerant parson quickly knows the basic questions essential to avoid an embarrassing disaster or, even worse, to prevent upsetting the parishioners whose sensitivity is barely skin deep.

"What do you normally expect me to wear?"

"You do what you like, padre."

That was not true. Get it wrong and you would be a marked man.

"Is the Sanctus sung or said?"

Assuming that they know what you are talking about, such an innocuous query can reveal much. In some churches, even the word "sanctus" must not be used; so another approach is required.

"What do you do here about the "Holy, Holy, Holy bit like?"

In fact the tradition of the particular church tends to be based on the ability of the organist. Long experience had taught me that the note offered by the organist could prove to be unacceptable and might be better ignored. That takes courage and would be better avoided by a quiet word before the Service with the lady on the harmonium.

Most organists claim to be pianists and, as that is exactly my problem with an organ, I was full of sympathy. The one attribute common to all organists is the love they have for their church, turning up Sunday after Sunday in spite of the sermons. Most played at an impossibly slow tempo and ended each verse with the lowest note on their machine. The next verse would then be preceded by another single note, which for the unwary would be taken as the beginning of the next line. For the innocent there are many pitfalls.

The better traps are kept for the visiting parson. The moment you set out from your clergy stall to tackle the next item from the lectern, an eye should be kept open for the character emerging from his pew, at a steady rate of knots, heading for the same lectern. It is not a race. You should have known that the gentleman in the fourth row back on the left always reads the Second Lesson on the Third Sunday in August. I had a technique to deal with this. I would stand at the lectern, give them a deep bow and return to my seat. They think you have afforded them a great honour and will give you a nod in return. The parson earns many Brownie points by doing this.

Some churches are vouchsafed a verger. They must be watched at all times. They tend to march purposefully towards you in the middle of a Psalm or the last but one verse of a hymn, bow deeply, about turn, elevate their wands and retreat. It is assumed that you should follow. Once I did this and set out in pursuit of the black-gowned verger. Then half way down the main aisle, he whipped around, gave a profound bow and took himself off. I did not know why I was there. Prayer is of little avail in such a dilemma, but help was at hand. A friendly female passed me her Book of Common Prayer and mouthed the word Litany. I got on with it. Half way through and going in grand style, a choirman leapt to his feet and, cutting me short, announced a hymn. God must find these Christian gymnastics as odd as the poor visiting parson does, but we are all doing our best.

My brand of churchmanship almost saw me in hospital, when I took my first Communion Service at St. Athanasius's. We are all a bit different when we enter the sanctuary with enough manual actions and body language to conduct an orchestra or stir a pudding.

It was my custom to genuflect at the consecration of the bread. I solemnly went down on one knee. It was agony. My right knee cap was being twisted out of place and an excruciating pain shot up my leg. I took off like sputnik and was surely airborne for a moment. There followed a dramatic silence as I dealt with the agony. When I continued, the congregation must have thought I was overcome by spiritual emotion.

The cause of my suffering was evident. The architect had placed a sharp knobbed paving around the altar and I had chanced upon his finest specimen, which I had rammed with my full twelve stone. There would be no more genuflections in that church!

As time went by, I was accepted as a human being and I began to appreciate the good folk of St. Athanasius. They were a kind and generous people and I realised that they were not being off-hand, but genuinely did not want to ask too much of me. The more that I asked of them, the more they achieved. They were good.

My sermons were brief and well laced with nautical anecdotes to which they could relate, most of them having Merchant Navy connections. We became friends.

The Church Wardens were adept at guiding me into homes where there was a need. In this way, I was led to a shop keeper, who was falling apart and the business with it. His problem was easy to diagnose, but the solution a little more difficult. His wife had died two years before and he was still not coping with the emptiness in his life. He was probably a man with a drink problem, rather than a man still grieving. Most had forgotten his wife and just saw a drunk.

At least once a week, I fell into the habit of calling in at lunch time, when the shop was shut and we could share a pot of coffee.

On those days, his first glass of whisky was postponed until the evening. He never knew which day I would call and began to gain control. Three families went out of their way to give quiet support and more importantly they began to make demands of him. He was elected treasurer of one organisation. That helped. There had been no fuss and no comment. When I eventually left Kirkdale, he put his arm about me and made it obvious that he had understood. In fact, it had been the community, which had brought him back to life and not just one individual.

In the height of that summer, those streets were warm and dusty. There was no grass anywhere for the children to tumble and play. Once again, by chance, I discovered that the women of Kirkdale were well able to handle such a situation. There was no need for expensive schemes and officialdom. Fortunately we were in the era when no-one had told us that we were deprived and that we should worry about our ethnic roots. Their answer was so simple that I almost missed it.

Every morning the children were taken along the roads to a park, armed with food and drinks and sticking plaster. Games were organised and every toddler was safe and happy. The simplicity of the scheme was that in the afternoon the available mothers on the other side of the street did their shift. In this way, the young mothers knew each other and could share their problems supporting each other. There were no lonely children!

I was not aware of any real tension over the religious divide between Catholic and Protestant, but it was always there like a ghost from the stormy past. We joked about it. Colour and ethnic back ground were irrelevant in our discussions, but full employment produced tolerance and there was no need for ghettos for the economically deprived. Perhaps we were comfortably blind.

Liverpool was equally divided fifty-fifty between Catholics and Protestants and was well served by the clergy of the day, who were learning the meaning of ecumenism in advance of the people in the parishes. The arrival of the "heavenly twins", Archbishop Derek Warlock and Bishop David Sheppard, was still a decade ahead.

They really were to show that life was better together.

I had never heard of Jelly Sunday, although it did sound interesting.

"Come and preach to our lot on Jelly Sunday."

My good friend, Ted, had to explain. He was a Vicar of a mid-Lancashire village some twenty-five miles outside Liverpool City.

"You'll enjoy it, Bob."

At the time that sounded like a threat. Actually it was a Sunday, when a number of villages came together for a walk and a spot of hymn singing. That done, they would all depart for their homes and there was no prize for guessing what was for afternoon tea.

I arrived in good time via the endless country lanes and sat in the car, waiting for the congregation to gather on the Village Green. It was a glorious summer day, sunshine, high clouds and a gentle breeze. The people appeared in their hundreds, all dressed in Sunday best. The youngest were dragged by hand, behind the marching brass bands. Animation increased as they reached the Green. Scattered around the arena were six ice-cream vans. They all played their jingles in competition with the church bells and against the three brass bands. The sound would have topped the charts today.

Clergy appeared from all directions and, at a nod from Ted, we shuffled forward, like penguins, as I was hoisted up with the Vicar onto the back of a hay cart. It was a splendid way to celebrate Whitsunday. The Vicar declared it a "right do". Kirkdale did it differently.

One Sunday we set out from the church in pursuit of the local Prize Silver Band, which was clearly in trouble trying to survive in the Rock and Roll era. They had done their best. Their peak caps had been handed down from generation to generation and the smallest lad had very little forward vision. But, they played with bravissimo and it was good to march along behind them.

We set out along Stanley Road, holding up the traffic and

disturbing those who had taken to their beds for a quiet Sunday afternoon's snooze. We threaded our way up and down the streets ... Crocus and Snowdrop, Pansy and Daisy, Woodbine and Harebell. Nothing could stop us.

The high spot for me was Daisy Street. The band led the way with the choir behind. Most of the choir lads wore cassocks knee high, variously hued and incredibly ancient. In contrast, the surplices were pure white, starched and ironed with the fervour only known to mothers. Some of the choristers were old and, like sheep dogs, these elderly gentlemen herded the dozen assorted children in front of them. They all sang merrily as the band pumped out the hymns. They were a great sight. We followed three paces back.

Immediately in front of me was the church banner. It was a big one, about ten feet high and four feet wide. It was kept aloft on a single pole, steadied by cords coming down to two out-riggers on either side. The Latin inscription was gold threaded. "Athanasius contra mundum." This was a brave challenge, Athanasius against the world! The doctrinal significance of that statement, which led to the Athanasian Creed was long lost, but that banner seemed to keep battle alive in Kirkdale.

Unfortunately, Albert, who was carrying the banner up Daisy Street, had an artificial leg. His side dipped as we meandered along. That was not all. As we turned into Daisy Street, the wind up graded and changed direction. This had a dramatic effect upon one of the more mature young ladies, who was one of the out-riggers. She must have borrowed for the occasion a pair of her mother's high heeled shoes. A heel came off! The result was dramatic and instant. The banner began to gyrate. If the following wind had been a mite stronger, they would have taken off like Mary Poppins.

I kept my dignity in a borrowed red cope with the Wardens on either side. I clasped my hands together, as in prayer, as we continued up Daisy Street. I nodded pontifically to all on-lookers and was beginning to get the hang of it.

Half way up on the left, a large lady sat outside her front door on a wooden kitchen chair. There never had been front gardens in these streets, in spite of the floral names. She sat with her legs well apart, displaying a splendid pair of elasticated bloomers. They were only of passing interest, until to my surprise she fixed me with her eyes and stuck out her tongue with a waggle of her head. Out of the corner of my mouth, I spoke to the Warden on my port .

"Hey, John, did you get that?"

"Ignore it , Bob. Give her a Protestant blessing."

So I half turned, made a dramatic sign of the Cross in her direction. She responded with a two finger salute. It was too much. I burst out laughing and winked. She winked back with a friendly nod. Ecumenical peace had been restored.

But we had not finished with Daisy Street. Not only were the people and the dust bins out, so were the dogs. I rather like dogs. Our uproarious cacophony had seen off every pigeon and seagull in the Kirkdale area, but we had forgotten the dogs. I became aware of a certain amount of blasphemy behind me. "Watch your back, padre!" It was a timely warning. Past me at a rate of knots, coming up from behind, emerged an excited, underfed mutt, who promptly cannoned into Albert and his banner. It had a tremendous effect; we all moved sideways. Just one man kept his cool. My starboard Warden could have played for Everton in his youth. Apparently he had always favoured his left foot. That dog was lifted in one swing towards the nearest dustbin. I have long forgotten what hymn we were singing at the time. All that I can recall with absolute clarity is a voice coming through from behind, "I bet that dog is a bloody Catholic!"

That interregnum in St. Athanasius Kirkdale had been an education and made me feel that Liverpool was my home.

12.

Eternal Father strong to save

For those in Peril

As the Port of Liverpool exploded in size, so the churches' interest in caring for the seafarer grew to meet the demand. The Non-Conformist Church was the first in the field, when they inaugurated, on the 12th September 1820, the Liverpool Seamen's Friend Society and in 1900 they built the splendid Gordon Smith's Institute. When I arrived in 1961, the Gordon Smith was still in action, used mainly by retired seamen, but in a few years it closed as it could not be modernised and lacked financial support.

In 1820, the Non-Conformists had acquired a ship for Liverpool and she was dubbed the Floating Chapel. The vessel was the two-decked "William", launched in Liverpool in 1775. She remained in the corner of Kings Dock until almost 1880, having accrued dock dues for twenty-eight years in the grand sum of £1,277.

The first Church of England Chaplain was the Reverend Dr. William Scoresby, M.A.,D.D.,F.R.S.(1789-1857). Scoresby was a brilliant sea Captain, an Arctic explorer and a scientist internationally known for his nautical studies. All this he left to take Holy Orders and, after a four year curacy in Bridlington, he came to Liverpool. At the end of 1825, he purchased the Frigate Tees, renamed her the Mariners' Church and moored her in the South-West corner of George's Dock. This warship had been in action under Nelson and had been commanded by Captain Marryat, R.N., the famous author. The Tees was to sink in George's

Dock after fifty years service in 1872. She had been able to accommodate a thousand strong congregation. Dr. Scoresby held regular services, which were mainly attended by seafarers, but also by local inhabitants. He visited all the ships in port, using his own boat. He was in Liverpool for five years, but when his wife became ill, he retired to Exeter.

His successor was the Reverend William Maynard and, whilst he worked hard and well, the initial impact of the Mariners' Church fell away and the seafarers ignored it. Maynard's ministry lasted forty years.

Liverpool at that time was a dangerous place for the seafarer. Too often he was robbed, beaten, drugged, befuddled with drink and shanghaied back to sea again before he had hardly set foot on dry land. The aim of the Institutions, like the Liverpool Sailors' Home, was to rescue the poor seafarer from the grog shops: "Drunk for a 1d and blind for 2d ... and the arms of women like Harriet Lane, Jumping Jennie and the Battle Ship!"

In the streets and alleys of dockland, there was no dearth of places where "Seamen's Lodging House" was painted boldly on the cracked, dirt-grained fanlight and where at exorbitant charge, the sailor would be fed and bedded ... after a fashion. The majority of boarding houses were poor establishments, from which some "shell back" (a sailor who had crossed the equator) was lucky to escape with his life, let alone his money belt.

In Liverpool Town Hall on the 18th October 1844, a public meeting was held and a committee formed. The Corporation offered a site and in a short time £13,600 was collected and the Liverpool Sailors' Home was under way. Liverpool was responding to the needs of the seafarer.

In 1850, the Government passed their Shipping Bill and to this day it is the basis on which crews are shipped and discharged. The next year, Schools for Nautical Instruction were opened and these were immediately adopted by the Board of Trade. In 1857, a School for Apprentices was started for instruction in reading, writing and arithmetic.

The Sailors' Home was destroyed by fire in 1860, but was quickly rebuilt. About this time there were forty-six public houses within two hundred yards radius of the Sailors' Home! That Home was to play a vital role, not only for the Mersey Mission to Seamen, but for other Societies as they were being founded.

When the Mersey Mission to Seamen in 1957 opened its new head-quarters in James Street at Pier Head, there was little hesitation in naming it Kingston House in memory of the author, philanthropist and founder of the Mersey Mission to Seamen. During my quarter of a century with the Mission, I was to complete Kingston House and eventually sell it in order to relocate the Mission at Seaforth. I believe that Kingston would have approved the courage and determination which these efforts were to demand. The Mission must always respond to needs and not to vested interest in buildings.

W.H.G.Kingston returned from a trip to Canada on the 30th January 1854. Two years later he was to found the Mersey Mission to Seamen. They were busy years. He produced two books, "Blue Jacket" and "A Chip off the Old Block". Apart from that, there was time to edit a number of books for boys. He also produced a well researched book of six hundred and fifty pages entitled "Western Wanderings".

In 1856 he returned from Russia and promptly arranged to visit Liverpool and Dublin. That journey was to take in Dublin, Kingstown, Cork, Queenstown, Waterford, Milford Haven and Liverpool. Just two days were spent in Liverpool, Saturday and Sunday, the 22nd and 23rd November 1856 and he sailed to Ireland on the Monday.

The details of this weekend are clearly recorded in a pamphlet, written in 1857, at a cost of four pence in a wrapper and sixpence in a cloth cover. It was entitled "A Cruise on the Mersey" or "Twelve Hours Missionary Work among Seamen with an account of the late proceedings of the Society for Promoting Missions to Seamen Afloat at Home and Abroad". A provisional committee, obviously the ground work had been well done, was called on the Saturday of people interested in seamen in Liverpool and a second meeting was arranged for the Monday, 24th November 1856. That was the first meeting and marks the founding of the Mersey Mission to Seamen.

So the Liverpool Mission was launched and, under the guidance of the London Missions to Seamen, the work started. At the beginning of 1858, the Reverend Bellamy was appointed at the instigation of London. Nothing is known about him and his stay was rather brief, because the first active chaplain seems to have been the Reverend Edward Thring.

These were the days of Brunel's Great Western and Thring would have visited her along with hundreds of ships on the river and in dock. Thousands of emigrants each month were leaving for the United States, which was opening up Westwards and also for the development of Canada. Thring believed in ship visiting and he set the pattern for the years ahead. He was found with the fishermen of Hoylake and with the canal families of Ellesmere Port. He battled with the Liverpool crimps and frequently was successful in taking men to the safety of the Sailors' Home, before they returned to their ships.

Thring left Liverpool in 1867 to serve in the Cincha Islands, off Peru, where guano was being worked. To care for men in such appalling conditions was a mark of the quality of the man. From Peru, Thring went to Uruguay and eventually, in old age, he returned home and became a curate of St. George's Church on Everton Brow. That was in 1874.

The work, well begun, continued. The Chaplains and the Readers visited the ships and established the need for daily contact with the seafarer. A major step was taken in 1874, when a room was rented in the Sailors' Home. We know that seven years previously one of the Chaplains was paid an extra £25 per annum for his work in the Sailors' Home. The final step was taken when in 1886 a Mission Building was placed on the corner of Hanover Street and Paradise Street, alongside the Sailors' Home. That new building was to become the Diocesan Headquarters in 1956, when the first stage of Kingston House was started.

Part of my task when I came to Liverpool in 1961, was to complete Kingston House by adding to Stage One a ten-storey hotel in 1963. The dramatic change in shipping and the decline in manning and the movement of the port to the North end, all combined into the decision to sell Kingston House in 1983 and move our headquarters some four miles to the North, alongside the Royal Seaforth Dock, into Colonsay House. So one hundred and ten years after renting a room in the Sailors' Home, the Mission is still well placed to continue the care for the seafarer.

There were dramatic changes in my time on Merseyside. I saw the closure of Atlantic House in Hardman Street. The work of the Roman Catholic Church is handled by the Apostleship of the Sea and, having started in 1925, after the closure of Atlantic House in 1983, everything is now centralised at the Stella Maris Club in the Strand at Bootle.

The Merchant Navy Welfare Board also closed their hotel in 1983, but have now withdrawn from Liverpool. The Liverpool Sailors' Home was demolished in the late sixties and now exists as a Trust Fund. The Gordon Smith Institute also went in the sixties.

Cleveland Street

Obviously the era of the big club was over. The demand for the provision of accommodation had almost ended, along with the almost total demise of the British Merchant Navy. The task for the Mission now is the care for the men from the Third World, which provides most of the modern seafarers.

Our care for the Lascars went back to the twenties with a club for Indian Seamen over the water in Cleveland Street, Birkenhead, and after the War we opened another similar establishment on Derby Road in Bootle. Indian films were shown most nights and over one hundred men appeared each evening. I closed both Clubs in the late sixties and centralised everything in Kingston House, as men from the sub-continent no longer felt the need for segregation. Indian films were no longer required.

Derby Road

The First Stage of Kingston House was opened by the Duke of Edinburgh in 1957. I arrived in 1961 just as we were closing Red Ensign House in Birkenhead, where we had cared for the thousands of men who had sailed from Merseyside in the tramping ships. Three years later, we closed our Merchant Navy Hotel for Officers and completed Stage Two of Kingston House.

I left the Mission in 1974 to become the Vicar of Rainhill in the Diocese of Liverpool, but was asked to return in 1979. Three men had followed me in rather quick succession. I came back to even more dramatic changes.

The revolution in ship handling and the size of the vessels and, above all, the great decline in manning levels meant that Kingston House was no longer the answer to the needs of the situation. A rear guard action to maintain the building was not necessary, as the work of the Mission is not dependent upon bricks and mortar. So we sold Kingston House and reorganised ourselves at Colonsay House, in the shadow of the Royal Seaforth Dock system. It quickly proved to be the right building in the right place. Many outsiders saw the closure of Kingston House as a sign of failure, but the story of the Mission and of the Port of Liverpool is one of the courage to adapt to and anticipate the present and future needs. In the end, this is our strength and why we need never fear the future.

Change is not without pain. Over fifty members of staff were made redundant when we closed Kingston House. D'rene and I lost our home. We ended up for a year in Mariners' Park in Wallasey, where we were well received, living in a two-bedroomed retirement bungalow. D'rene accepted the need for the Mission to survive and part of the cost was over half of our furniture had to be given away. We survived. Selling Kingston House was not simple, as we were in the Hatton era, and Liverpool was not apparently viable. But, Liverpool survived too!

13.

ALPHA OMEGA   ALPHA OMEGA
MEGA ALPHA OMEGA   ALPHA
OMEGA   ALPHA OMEGA   ALPH
MEGA   ALPHA OMEGA ALPHA
OMEGA   ALPHA OMEGA AL
PHA OMEGA   ALPHA   OMEG

Which God?

The most important advance for all the organisations involved in caring for the seafarer was the launching of the International Christian Maritime Association (ICMA). It enabled us to approach our activities ecumenically, in honest friendship, and ensured that never would we have to compete against each other in our world-wide commitments. Today there are Mission stations around the world, where Chaplains of differing denominations share the same altar, the same building and the same motivation ... and, of course, the same God!

It was Sookie Paterson, at the ICMA Plenary Conference in 1985, speaking specifically about ministry to Korean seafarers, who expressed the motivation in plain language.

"If I speak with the tongue of Korean seamen but do not have love, I have become a noisy gong or a clanging cymbal. And if I have a Seamen's Centre and know all knowledge about ships and seamen, but do not have love, I am nothing. Build a bridge of love from your heart to the seamen's hearts, and let Jesus walk across."

This says it all, but opens up the entire question: "Which God are we representing in our ministry?"

We cannot really assess the population figures in the world, but in 1965, the guestimate for the total world population was given as 4,700 millions and an overall estimated religious count was given to try to present a picture of the faiths in the world.

Christianity	:	1,500 millions
Islam	:	820 millions
Hinduism	:	650 millions
Buddhism	:	300 millions
Judaism	:	14 millions
Sikhism	:	16 millions
Atheism	:	210 millions
Tribalism	:	90 millions

Early in this century, there has been an attempt to Westernise Islam, but as we all have observed in the last decade or so, the growth of the Ayatollahs has moved Islam into extreme fundamentalism, pushing all hope of ecumenism aside.

Islam began in Mecca about A.D.610. Muhammad was born in Mecca about A.D.570 and at the age of forty he believed that he was receiving messages from God. These were collected and formed the Koran. God (Allah) was One, merciful, all powerful, controlling the world. On the last day there would be the judgement. His followers, the Muslim, were persecuted and so Muhammad in A.D.622 travelled to Medina - this marked the beginning of the Islamic Era. There the Prophet developed his religion - worship, prayer, almsgiving and a pilgrimage to Mecca were the basics. Also legal regulations were formulated for the Arab world.

Muhammad's followers grew in strength, mainly in the face of Judaism. The Prophet died in A.D.632. He left a religion and a state, which rapidly expanded by conquest into Egypt, Syria and Iraq. In the next century, the Muslims took all North Africa through to Spain, then Turkey, Persia, Afghanistan and into Pakistan. There expansion stopped, apart from a gradual influx into India. This remained the area of Islam up to the eighteenth century.

Then the religion spread again to Malaysia, Indonesia, the Philippines and Eastern China. The explosion of Christianity in the nineteenth century barely touched Islam, but the economic growth and the social demands of the Muslims were growing.

Today the Muslims base their industrial growth on the Western models and they have taken full control of their oil fields. They are very aware of the need to capture the soul of Africa, but we live in an age of secularism and in the newly independent African States, where there are large Muslim populations, radical reforms appear to be reducing Islam to the status in which we find Christianity in this country. I suspect that Islam is not prepared to accept that.

Islam, the largest religion in the Middle Ages, is on the march again. It is militant. The mass demonstrations that we see on our television screens cannot be compared with the gentle hand-shaking exodus from our parish churches on Sundays.

Sadly, the form of Christianity, which we presented to the Empire and the world in the last century, was firmly associated with imperialism and economic domination. Even though we can with justice defend the White Raj and point out its immense contribution to the peoples, we cannot remove that stigma from our brand of Christianity. Islam views our faith with suspicion.

Twentieth century Islam is evolving, but has the problem of its fundamentalists. The doctrine of holy war (jihad) calls upon Muslims to wage war in order to bring the non-Muslim world under the dominance of Islam. No Muslim nation can join the United Nations Organisation with that doctrine! Again, Islamic law prescribes the death penalty for a Muslim who apostasizes from Islam. They have watered down the demand for stoning for adultery, the amputation of the hand for stealing and flogging for other offences. Although the Koran prohibits usury, they now have accepted the need for rates of interest, banks, stocks and shares and other financial customs.

I wonder how many young men at the end of the war, expected that people would then wish to live in peace and brotherhood with each other. It did not happen. At the time of the Falkland affair, we were told that there were at least forty potential trigger points in the world and that, if we did not respond firmly to the Argentine invasion, there could be a domino effect in the world. There was more than a grain of truth in that. Nation still hates nation and, yet, I believe that in our generation there has been a change for mankind such has never been experienced before.

We in this country are now living in a world community, whether we like it or not, and we have not yet come to terms with it. Some of us hope that it will go away! Leicester is the largest Hindu centre outside India. There are more Muslims than Methodists in Britain. There are more Jews per square mile in Redbridge than you would find in Israel. Southall is the new capital city for the Sikhs. The peoples of the world are spreading around the world. People of all nations are living in our country. It is a process in which we are becoming one people, one nation across the world, and, if we fail to absorb that fact, we might tear our nation apart. The basic change in our lifetime is that we live within one day and a half from every other person in the world.

Sometimes I feel that God's plan for the world is far more simple than we realise. The basis of that plan has been with us for almost two thousand years and it is being implemented around us whether we approve or not. The plan is that, if you cannot live together as nations, then nations will split up and we will learn to live together as neighbours. That is precisely the challenge that we are facing in Britain

A telephone call from the principal of Riversdale Technical College put the matter into perspective.

"The nautical students from Iran are demanding that a room be set aside for their regular prayers."

I explained that these young men were watching each other and that, even so far from home, they were expected to conform with the religious demands of Islam.

In our terms, these young cadets were living under intimidation, a concept entirely alien to our thinking. Our Christianity seems to put us under little religious obligation and no-one appears to worry whether you have a faith at all. This gives us no right to tell others how to conduct themselves, although we have the right to think and have an opinion. As I write, there is a photograph in a newspaper showing two bodies hanging head-down from a gantry in Iran, as "an encouragement to others". Sadly, there are too many historical examples of like activity in our faith!

Lunch aboard an Indian ship was never to be refused. It was always an experience! Some time was to elapse before I discovered that "ladies fingers" on the menu was nothing to worry about; it was just another odd vegetable. The real challenge and concern was the colourful collection of sauces, bottles and dishes of mysterious condiments and explosive substances, sitting like a Modern Tate exhibit in the middle of the mess table. The Golden Rule was " Never to help yourself", and the corollary followed, "When in doubt, don't". I have observed many a guest, trained in the Tandoori Taj Mahal restaurant in Birkenhead or some such place, reach with confidence for a multi-coloured pot, ladle a spoonful as though it was concocted by Bransons and, then, with all the Indian eyes gazing in wonder at his courage, barely survive the meal as he was rendered permanently speechless. Another Golden Rule is "Always seek advice". Quickly I learned that the only way to tackle a curry was with a spoon and a fork ... a little at a time. Keep the jug of water in front of you.

Meat was ever difficult. Never assume that you are eating chicken or lamb or beef or that the Chief Officer is any wiser than you are ... some questions are better not asked.

Having played behind a rugby scrum was invaluable training to block the smiling steward coming up on your blind side and intent on ladling a strange yellow liquid over your mound of rice. It is better not to inquire as to what is lurking in that rice.

You were a happy man, if you had no idea as to what was going on or rather up, behind you! So many ships were home to the ever present cockroach. One just assumed that they loved the galley and then promptly obliterated that thought out of your mind. They always appeared in racing pairs, edging up the bulkhead behind the person in front of you, making conversation difficult. It would have been fun to place bets on the field, but their presence was not to be mentioned.

The pudding was always the same ... icecream. It was served in plastic cartons, which had circum-navigated the globe a number of times and they often showed signs of wear. I never asked about the dearth of glass dishes. One peach slice sat on top to give the icecream a smile. I wondered how they had the ability to disguise the scraggiest of necks to resemble a sort of venison and then run out of ideas for puddings!

The main challenge then followed. The first time that I faced this particular surprise was on a Jala boat, when the Chief Engineer leapt to his feet and re-appeared carrying a plastic bag full of bird seed. I was wrong, of course, having ignored yet another Golden Rule for Survival in Indian Ships, "Never jump to a conclusion". I should have known that the Chief was not "into bird seed". The plastic bag held flower seeds. He explained.

"These are what I take when I return to my cabin". It did not seem much of an explanation to me, except to indicate that he was a flower seed addict.

"Put some in your hand and then pop them into your mouth, but whatever you do, please not to swallow whatever."

This was a clear warning and instinct told me that another Golden Rule was in the making, but the memory of Tommy Handley took over, so I countered with "After you!" His name was not Claud, but Sing. He smiled.

"Let me further advise you that you must chew them into a ball in your mouth and then, after a suitable passage of time, deposit them on your plate."

He spoke like Lord Tonypandy with a singing lilt in rounded English. This is why we Welsh get along remarkably well with Indian crews. Faced with the plastic bag, there was no escape, so I did as advised and partook of the flower seeds. It was an experience never to be forgotten and certainly not to be discussed in hearing of the drug squad! Strange and wonderful aromas seemed to pervade my being and I reckoned that I was on a trip. We spoke about many things like marigolds and poppies. In the end, I was saved by their indescribable coffee with its shot of condensed milk, which I assumed on that occasion came to us by courtesy of carnations!

Many times I comforted myself with the thought that I was aboard, not for the food, but for the cut and thrust of human conversation and, with luck, the odd reference to God. All the meals started with a can of some foreign beer, although out of courtesy for the cloth, I was given the ship's glass. All lunches aboard those ships were tremendous fun, gentle leg-pulling and fascinating discussion. It was a privilege to be with them.

Over the meal, I was invariably told that Indian civilisation went back well past five thousand years and it was inferred that my Welsh tribe would have been running around in animal Y-fronts, hitting each other about the head with clubs and painting all our moving parts purple. They made it sound like a rugby match against the English at Cardiff Arms Park. All of this was a touch disconcerting to a man taught in school that anything East of Turkey was over-curried and that it was us that had taken civilisation into the world. I suspect that mine is the last generation to be influenced by the British Empire, when half the plates in a Macmillan Atlas was coloured red and the other bits were occupied by ignorant foreigners. Lunches can be very enlightening.

Hinduism (the Persian word for Indian) is the third largest religion in the world. It has taken five thousand years to evolve and the word Hinduism was only coined in A.D.1100, when the Muslims wanted to distinguish their own activities. Hinduism has no founder, no prophet, no particular ecclesiastical structure, nor a set creed. It is a way of life, rather than a way of thought, more a culture than a creed. Hinduism is concerned with India, the land, the social system, the history ... it is about Mother India. The rivers are regarded as the source of life, especially the Ganges, which epitomises "life without end". The sacred city is Varanasi on the Ganges and is the best place chosen for dying. After cremation, the ashes are to be cast upon the waters of the sacred river and this enables life to continue. Not all Hindus would believe in God! Hinduism is like an umbrella which embraces many religious beliefs. The fundamental thought is that life will continue through many existences, reincarnation with birth, death and rebirth. All this removes any sense of urgency about making a decision about anything.

In my life-time, the whole concept of Hinduism has been influenced by Mahatma Gandi, who in his life-style embraced the denial of the world's riches and gave his life for political freedom and the recognition of his people. That is why, in the presence of Hindus, I felt a deep sense of calm and gentle acceptance as we chatted together. There was none of the aggression and self-centredness found so readily in Western society. We tend to assert our own importance at the expense of others. This is not the Indian way. Gandi put it very simply and yet profoundly when he said, "My life is my message". We have much to learn from each other.

Normally when I arrived on a ship, I would hole out in a cabin. Word quickly went the rounds that the padre was aboard and, in no time, the cabin was full, men on the floor and on the bunk. I was given the only chair. Conversation flowed, not manipulated by me. There was little inhibition as to the subjects to discuss and I never found a better way to make time stand still.

During one visit a seafarer jumped to his feet to make his point and claim our attention.

"You Ishmael, you Ahmed, you Bob, you Gupta. All different. But must be one God for all!"

Then we talked and gave each other the glimpse of God that we each shared. There was no room for arrogance or bigotry or spiritual pride in that opening of the heart. All that we could conclude was to admit to each other that we all "saw through a glass darkly". That was an honest conclusion! So many times I have sat in conferences and been lectured at by extremely wise men, as they have dispensed their particular brand of wisdom and I have longed to be back in the company of those men from the corners of the earth, who were saying in their own way, "If your life is not your message, then you have no message".

In many ways, the Sikhs were the easiest people to come alongside. Their religion originated in Pakistan and in the Punjab about the end of the fifteenth century, at a time when Islam and Hinduism were firmly rooted. It answered a need for a more ritualistic and formal approach to God and led to a way of life that belonged to the ethnic group called the Sikhs.

Their religion, as with Judaism, became the community and where people went, so did the religion. God existed to be worshipped and above all to be understood. This was to result in a mystical and meditative approach to God. The Gurus were the Holy Men, who interpreted God to the people. In the sixteenth century, they built the famous Golden Temple at Amritzar, which became the centre for the Sikh religion and thus for the national life. It was to symbolise all that they held sacred. In the 1960's, there was a great change of attitude amongst the Sikhs around the world and, in our country, it led to the building of temples and a positive endeavour to create a Sikh community here. The aim is to bind the people together into a family. We would be completely wrong if we were to ask them to integrate with us and forget that they were a self-contained religious community. Integration would destroy them. There is no way in which a member of the Sikh community can be separated from his religion and remain a Sikh. Their religion is no threat to any other religion. I saw my task as simply walking together and learning from each other, as we journey both with and towards God.

Siddharta Gautama was born about 560 B.C. and was later known as Buddha. Many stories were woven around his birth and life. He was born in North East India amongst a people steeped in Hinduism. His religion challenged the spirituality of India. It was a strange mixture of belief. The Hindu writings were rejected, the caste system was abandoned and also the idea of God as a superior being. The religion almost allowed one to be an atheist! No wonder

A Dog Collar in the Docks

Buddhism failed to flourish in India! Buddha is regarded as an ordinary human being, although he stood above all other men and presented a challenge for man to seek enlightenment. It is difficult to describe a religion that lacks the ties of religion. It seems wrong to say that Buddhism aims to lead you into a "state of nothingness", yet that is near the truth. It became the religion of China, Tibet, Japan, Korea and South East Asia. Above all the ideology seems able to flirt with Marxism. I found it hard to convey to the Buddhists that as Christians we believe in a positive life with God at work within us and that we look for forgiveness and new life in Jesus. We are truly worlds apart.

There was one exciting month in the Mission when a Japanese priest from Tokyo came to stay with us. He was a member of the small Anglican Church in Japan, a country where Christians of any breed are few. Daniel Satou tried to explain to us the mixture of religions in Japan and even gave us an hour's seminar every morning in an attempt to educate us. It came across as a Confucian, Buddhist and Shintoistic mix and I sensed that his Christianity seemed to embrace the lot! Japan has been secularised, but the people still hang on to the various festivals from all the religions and from their folk memory ... much the same is happening in our country.

Visiting a Japanese ship was a pleasing experience. We were always well and politely received, but it was not until Daniel Satou came aboard with me that I understood what was happening. I had been made welcome because I was the local padre. They expected me to call and nothing was too much to please me. I enjoyed all that. However, Daniel was Japanese and was almost totally ignored when we were together. I assumed that it was because he was a Christian. Once again Christianity was being treated as a Western affair and nothing to do with Japan.

Until the Christian congregations around the world are able to produce, over many generations, an indigenous priesthood, our faith will be judged as peculiar to us and of little interest to them. The Good News must be seen in our lives.

Our baptisms were different

In the Mission I felt that we knew how to open doors for dialogue. We took the first step and went to them. The second step was when they came to our place. That established the bond of friendship. The third step was when both sides accept in their hearts that there can only be one God and that we can share our mutual knowledge of Him.

I knew where I stood as a Christian and I never felt at risk as I met men of other faiths. This was not bigotry. It seemed to me that God was working through all our imperfections and that He will sort us out.

Spiritual experiences can be shared and a faith which cannot be "knocked about a bit" is not much of a faith! My observation was that, whilst Christianity is in institutional decline in Europe, it is flourishing in Africa, Latin America and East Asia. Communism has failed to remove it in Russia and China.

Sadly, we all tend to put the other man's religion down, but as I was actually meeting men who really practised their faith, there was no way in which I could write them off because I chanced to be a Christian. One way to deal with this dilemma is to say that Christianity is just our path to God, neither better nor worse than many others. However, we read in the Bible that Jesus asked us to go out to all nations with the truth about Him.

I believed that in my work with seafarers I was looking for echoes and reflections of the Spirit of Jesus in men of all faiths. This was what Jesus did. He accepted people as they were and dealt with their problems as they were. He passed judgement on all established religion ... the Pharisees, the Scribes and the leaders of religion in Jerusalem. He did this because He was looking beyond established religion to find God working in man. This surely means that we are to accept other faiths, where they fill out, underline and use a new vocabulary about the Glory of God. It can only be the same Glory that we accept from our knowledge of Jesus. There is only one Glory! We must reject other faiths, when that Glory is not revealed in the actions and thinking of their adherents. This need for rejection must also apply to the followers of Christ, when their lives fall short of the Glory of God. I am certain that this is the way to live with the religions of the world. Not one of us can go wrong, if we are truly attempting to open our lives and our minds to the Glory of God.

14. Ashore

A letter from Mr. Van Hooten of the Royal Seamen's Pension Fund in London alerted Jacqueline Wylde of the Mercantile Marine Service Association in Wallasey, which was already giving a small grant to a family, that there was a need for a padre to make a personal visit. That was to be me.

This is a perfect example of the quality of co-operation between the various Seafaring Charities on Merseyside and beyond. My main task and that of the staff was to respond immediately to any request for personal visits. The dog collar opens every door. The aim was to discover the need and then tap it into the Societies who could meet it.

So I visited Jane at her second floor flat, just off Mill Street, in the notorious Liverpool 8 area. Normally I went alone, trusting that the dog collar would afford all the protection that I needed. It was not possible to drive the car right up to the tower block because of the debris of bricks and broken glass, which covered the road. It was clear that the area was being deliberately run down, as it screamed of neglect and demolition. In a few years those blocks were to be replaced with good houses, but in the meanwhile there were still families living there. Leaving the car outside a pub, which stood in splendid isolation like an oasis of civilisation, I ignored the lift and climbed the smelly staircase to the second floor.

The flat was spotless and the welcome genuine, although the carpets and curtains were very tired. It was a sad story. Jane's husband had died ten years previously after serving for some fifty years in the Merchant Navy. Four years ago, Jane's daughter had died suddenly at the age of thirty-one, leaving a boy and a girl. The children's father proved to be incapable of caring for them and he disappeared, abandoning the family and leaving the grandmother to cope on her own. She had real problems, but had struggled on alone.

I arrived on the very day that she received a letter from the Director of Housing stating that she had been given a new home on the other side of Mill Lane. This was wonderful, the answer to the needs of the family, and it had made my visit all the more necessary.

My first discovery was that Jane was not receiving all the financial support from the State to which she was entitled. That was quickly and easily rectified. She had unbelievably been supporting herself and the two youngsters on her widow's pension and the family allowance. It was a happy home, the children were fit and well, and I could not praise Jane highly enough for all that she was doing.

The D.H.S.S. increased her pension with a supplementary allowance of £13.63 per week; this was January 1987. As Jane had no legal standing as a guardian, I assumed that that was all that the State could provide. The grand-daughter was sixteen and the grand-son was twelve and both were at school. I contacted the Sailors' Children Society in Hull, knowing that they would respond. Because of her level of income, she did not have to meet rent or rates at that time. The urgent need was carpet and curtaining as she was due to move on the first of February. This was a situation tailor-made for the Ship-wrecked Mariners' Society, which was based in Chichester and for whom we acted as the agent on Merseyside. The General Secretary was Valerie Austin and as we had built up a trust over the years, I knew that the response would be swift. Urgent decisions can always be endorsed by committees at a later date.

Miss Austin asked for a list of needs. Obviously coming from a flat, there was a requirement for carpets in the hall, on the staircase and landing. Jane had decided that she would occupy the smallest bedroom with a single bed and a chair, leaving the larger rooms for the children. The grand-daughter's room needed eight square yards of carpet and a chair and table for her studies. The dining area in the kitchen, just ten feet square, needed carpet. A washing machine seemed essential. The three piece suite was in bad condition and there was little else in the lounge. The house had central heating, which was wonderful for Jane and she had ordered a gas-fire on hire purchase, which we paid for in full. My eyes told me that the grand-son was in need of new clothes and this was sorted out quietly.

The response was excellent. The Ship-wrecked Mariners' Society gave an immediate initial grant, which clothed both children. The Sailors' Children's Society provided the washing machine, which we organised. My request for all the furnishings and carpets was completely met by King George's Fund for Sailors.

K.G.F.S. is really an umbrella organisation "supporting by medium of a central fund, organisations existing for the help, comfort and relief of seafarers and their dependants and they achieve this by maintaining an effective fund raising organisation". This latter role was undertaken in the North-West by Sally Atherton. I had no hesitation in putting Jane's situation to Sally and, whilst K.G.F.S. is unable by its charter to give direct assistance, she found a way to unravel the problems. Sally never failed with her help and support.

At last, Jane's income was supplemented correctly and I knew that she was able to maintain the standards aimed for by all the helping agencies.

Until I retired some three years later, I visited Jane regularly, often with D'rene alongside, and we all enjoyed a cup of tea together. This was the way to keep an eye on the situation and we were delighted with the progress of the children.

An equally regular visitor was my secretary, Pat Ball, as she like us felt part of the Mission's extended family. In one report, Pat wrote that "Jane works very hard to provide a comfortable environment for her grand-children and they are very proud of her. A charming lady to interview. Her home is well cared for by her. She is a great lady!" All that was a long way from the situation when I had made my first visit. I will never forget her.

In most of the back streets of Liverpool, you will find the four-storey Victorian houses, which in London are priceless, but on Merseyside are warrens for bed-sits. Alex lived in one on the second floor. Parking the car on yet another littered street, I faced the staircase, dark, uncarpeted and smelling of urine and debris.

Alex had three locks on his door and still did not feel secure. You walked straight into his bedroom, no carpet, no window, lit by a bare bulb. The bed was covered by coats and was not clean. Through the bedroom was the kitchen with its high Victorian window, some twelve feet from floor to ceiling. There was a sink unit with an electric ring on the draining board. A wire stretched behind the taps to the electric plug on the wall. This was where Alex did his cooking and boiled a saucepan of water for his tea. The only furniture was an old table and two wooden chairs. All his food and possessions were kept on the table. There was nothing else except a one bar electric fire ... the only means of heating anywhere ... and he trailed it on a long flex from the kitchen to the bedroom. Alex was in his mid-seventies, a seafarer all his working life, and whilst he was doing his best, he was not succeeding in keeping himself fed or warm. There had to be a better way of survival for him than this slow death in Upper Parliament Street.

I was hopeful that I could convince him that he would be more comfortable and secure in Gateacre Grange. The Grange was a splendid establishment for retired seafarers, run by our Roman Catholic friends, the Apostleship of the Sea. I knew the place well and had no doubt that he would be completely at home.

Alex was not convinced. In his own time and at his pace, Alex eventually paid a visit to the Grange. He had a free bus pass and I felt that he had to make the moves and decision without any pressure from me.

As I feared, Alex decided to stay in Upper Parliament Street. He said that he wanted his independence, although there would have been no question of losing it at the Grange. That was his choice and it had to be honoured, though I felt deeply sorry for him. He refused all help. He remained with no radio, no television and, as far as I could see, no friends.

Alex had his dreams. He was born in Newfoundland and, on his behalf, I wrote a number of letters trying to trace his family, but the trail was long lost. At least the search brought him into the Mission fairly regularly, which enabled us to give him food and a hot drink and keep an eye on him. Perhaps in the end, we were giving him all that he wanted from us and the sense of failure was only in our minds. Too many seafarers die alone in the back streets!

Pat Ball, together with Simon, one of our student helpers, at the request of the Warden of a newly built sheltered housing complex in Bootle, called to visit Larry. He was a retired seaman, aged seventy, a widower and a loner. The Liverpool Housing Association, whose manager, Les Bradshaw, was a personal friend over many years, had produced an excellent property and Larry had been rescued from the loneliness of his home after the death of his wife. He had stopped caring for himself and his old home had been in a bad shape. The Housing Association had rescued him just in time.

Larry now lived in a splendid one bedroom flat. There were well furnished communal rooms in which to meet the other residents and a first class lunch was available every day in the central dining room. Above all, Larry had his own front door key and retained his vital privacy. But, it was not working. The Warden realised that this old seafarer was not responding to his new environment. Pat was to be the answer.

Pat could bring a smile to the most miserable of our customers; Larry was to be her ultimate challenge. Larry was just a sad man and was visibly failing. His only child, a daughter, had emigrated to Australia some years before. He was in deep despair. In fact he clung to Pat and broke down. Pat calmed him and proceeded to make the inevitable cup of tea, which buys you time to get your act together. Simon, the student, was struck dumb!

They talked about his life, his wife and his daughter and his despair. Even his television was on the blink! The whole world seemed stacked against him. He was well into the despond of self-pity and nothing is more destructive.

Pat became a regular visitor along with the rest of us and with the ever ready help of the Shipwrecked Mariners' Society, we bought a new bed, two arm chairs and, of course, a television. All this caring helped Larry settle into his new home and slowly he became part of his new family and rejoined the human race.

We quietly eased ourselves out, knowing that the Warden would alert us if he was in further difficulty. Larry was as happy, eventually, as the proverbial lamb.

I owed much to the foresight and interest of Lionel Storrs, who was Chairman of the Liverpool Sailors' Home Trust. Lionel suggested that we took over the local agency for the Shipwrecked Mariners' Society, which had been handled previously by the Sailors' Home. It was a move which added dramatically to the work of the Mission. Whilst we continued caring for the serving seafarer, we were as a result of the agency able to be much more effective in our work with the retired man and his family.

Hugh was a typical retired seaman, who had never established any roots. Whilst sea-going, he had not owned a home, but had moved from lodging house to lodging house. He was a bachelor whose life had been the sea. At last, in his early sixties, he was given the tenancy of a Corporation flat and his problems started.

It is unfair to suggest that such a man is improvident and that he should have saved for his retirement. The cost of board and lodge had eaten his money, which he had earned in his career. Like every seaman there had been many gaps when there were no berths available for him ... no ship, no work, no money! Such a person drifts into retirement, still believing that tomorrow would bring a ship and then all would be well. At last it would dawn upon the man that there would be no more sea-going. He wakes up to the fact that his monies had run out and that his working life was over. Hugh, like so many before him, had arrived "on the beach". Pat described him as a "king with no riches".

The new Council flat brought delight into his life. This was the big chance at last. All that he possessed was packed into two suit-cases! Then he thought about his problem ... not that much thought was required. Hugh had nothing, not even a knife and fork! The Social Services had contacted us about Hugh and we worked together against the clock. The aim was to install him on the Friday, three days ahead.

We had an "immediate grant" from the Shipwrecked Mariners' Society, a D.H.S.S. grant, there was the Church Resource Centre and ourselves. I could hardly believe what can be achieved with a small amount of money and everyone's co-operation.

> The cooker cost £75, inclusive of fitting.
>
> The bed ... £25.
>
> Three piece suite ... £45.
>
> Table and four chairs ,,, £25
>
> Carpets throughout ... £80.
>
> Coffee table ... £20.
>
> Food cabinet ... £20.
>
> Pots, pans, cutlery etc. ... £25

The rest of the bits and pieces were in our cellar, including a television. I was impressed by the efficiency of our staff.

Hugh was safely installed on the Saturday and seemed to enjoy playing house. Happily he cooked and cleaned and I knew that he was no longer a threat to himself and would not be a burden on society.

"Please pop in for a cup any time!"

That was all the thanks that we needed. Hugh had safely "swallowed the anchor".

The Toxteth Law Centre alerted me to the needs of an Indian seaman with the name of Mohammed. He had called at the Centre with all the problems in the world and naturally they were to become ours. It was not going to be easy. Mohammed lived in the heart of the notorious Liverpool 8. Yet again, I set out alone with my dog collar to the fore.

It was never admitted that Liverpool 8 was a "no-go" area for the police, but, the week previously, a police car had called off its pursuit rather than go in alone. Also, the owner of a jewellery shop had complained in the Press about the lack of protection. All I had was my dog collar.

I failed to get any response from the Victorian house where Mohammed lived. There were at least a dozen buttons to press and I tried them all, but no-one answered. Finally, I pressed for Mohammed again and decided to wait a long time. At last the door opened.

Mohammed was eighty-five years old and seemed barely alive to me. He had struggled down two flights of stairs and it was obvious why it had taken him ten minutes. He was unwell, short of breath and walking with pain. The climb back up was difficult and slow. Conversation was impossible.

The day was cold and icy and I kept my coat on in his bed-sit. I knew that it was not going to be easy to decipher his confusion and unravel his finances, but my time was his and I was not to hurry. It took him a long time to get his breath, whilst I made a cup of tea.

His clothes were clean and he had washed and shaved. We sat on wooden chairs either side of the table in the kitchen, which served as dining room and lounge. The place was spotless. He explained that a home-help came twice a week and "meals on wheels" arrived every day, except on Sunday. This food was Indian-style and looked totally unappetising ... he agreed with my diagnosis. It still sat in the sink, a cold and congealed mess. In fairness, I suspected that he had long lost interest in food. There was little of it in the kitchen and I opened every cupboard. He assured me that he chose to eat out three times a week, a real treat, and that was enough for him.

We talked well together and I thoroughly enjoyed hearing this eighty-five year old Indian seafarer talking about his life in the early coal burning ships. He had worked all his life on British ships for British owners. When I hear people pontificating that this sort of person should go back home, I feel very annoyed. Mohammed had given all his working life to this country and, as far as I could see, he had received very little reward of the good things in life. His language was a mixture of Indian, Scouse and the incomprehensible.

My main concern was his bedroom. The old house had been converted into many flatlets. The ceiling was too high, so the room was very cold. The heat was provided by a 1930 type two bar electric fire. One bar was hanging down, almost unattached, and was obviously dangerous. He was drying his washing on a chair in front of this fire. The bedding was clean, but inadequate as he used his top coat as an extra blanket.

I enjoyed the visit and he so clearly was equally pleased to see me. He had been able to talk about all the things which were important to him. All seafarers love talking, but rarely find anyone who is interested enough to ask the right questions.

I was able to call back a number of times and we provided him with a safe convector heater and a bundle of blankets. But that initial visit was not quite over!

As I left him that first time, he gave me the blessing of Allah and not to be out-faced I reciprocated in my style. We left it to God to sort out that particular confusion, although I suspect that both blessings were acceptable.

Back in the street, I turned the car and rounded the corner. Suddenly an on-coming car swung across in front of me and in the mirror I saw another had pulled up tight behind. I was trapped. There was no place to go. I wound down the window, stuck my head out and hopefully revealed my dog collar. I shouted, "Good afternoon". Two non-Caucasians appeared from the car behind me.

"What are you doing here, man?"

I calmly explained about my visit to Mohammed and gave the address. I talked about the problem of being eighty-five, infirm and Indian and what I intended to do to help him. They smiled. We pumped palms and with a wave they backed off.

I probably hold the Liverpool 8 speed record for a standing start from nought to sixty. On reflection, it was the only time that I really felt threatened in that area.

There had been one occasion when I had left a student in the car, whilst I made a visit. He was meant to guard the vehicle! When I returned, the car was surrounded by youths and contained a very frightened young man. He was a few years later ordained and came to work in the heart of Liverpool, so the experience had not put him off Merseyside.

I shall not forget Brian. The headline in the Liverpool Echo said it all.

"Seaman in horror cash bid".

The article was written by Anne Harrison. Brian was on a chemical tanker, about the enter a Turkish port, when the ship's line to a tug snapped. It lashed across Brian's legs. He lost the lower part of his right leg and the left leg was amputated below the knee. Eventually Brian returned home to Kirby and the complex legal battle for compensation started.

He was only entitled to a third of his pay until the April, then he would be signed off the firm's books and would not be entitled to redundancy or lay-off money. He worked for a Norwegian Shipping Company. The National Union of Seamen and the Knowsley

North Labour M.P., George Howarth asked the Transport Secretary, John Moore, to press for fair compensation.

The accident happened in the January and in the middle of the year the third child was born. Here was a lovely family and we were able to obtain grants from various sources. Obviously the settlement would take a long time.

Not once did we hear this brave man complain and my secretary, Pat Ball, thought he was the most courageous man she had ever met. His wife was charming and with the care of three children, the home was beautiful. We all thought that it was a privilege to visit and we hoped that we were of some value to this remarkable family. Brian battled on!

Whilst it was my task to make the initial visit to many homes, much of the ground work was then carried forward by Pat with the help of students. These young men did the driving and ensured that she was safe. We usually had two students at a time and just the once there was a young lady called Rachel. She was good until she fell in love with an officer cadet ... and then she was brilliant!

Many students, after a fortnight, did not hesitate to tell each one of us how the work should be done, but we had long learned how to respond with understanding smiles. Most of them in time proved to be a great strength and, when they departed a year later, they confessed that they had grown a little wiser. Some were to be ordained a few years later and all were to thank us for allowing them the opportunity to meet men from all over the world. Actually they kept us on our toes!

Behind all the activity in the Mission was Les Gunn, the Company Secretary. Les had come to us from the Mersey Docks and Harbour Company, via the Middle East, and brought calm and commonsense with his skills of administration.

When the office was filled with half a dozen retired seamen of mixed nationalities, Les always gave a hand. It was not unusual in mid-morning to find Les, Pat and myself in different corners of the Mission filling forms in triplicate.

Each interview could take an hour as we battled with the language barrier. The more we inquired about money, the more the language gulf widened. Too often a house visit was necessary to check that the seventy year old retired Asian seafarer really had three children under the age of ten. The wives were often in their twenties and I quietly wondered how many other wives were tucked away. The homes were spotless and the children well dressed.

It was a happy day when we met Mohammed Aden Saeed, a sixty year old seafarer, born in British Somaliland, which at the time was a British Protectorate. Saeed joined his first ship in Bombay at the age of eighteen and for the whole of his sea-going career, he sailed in British owned ships. His life had been hard. In those days, a fireman had to be a tough and resilient character. He started as a fireman, then a greaser, a donkey greaser and finally a storekeeper.

Saeed was at sea from 1946 to 1979. He came to Britain in 1947 and, in order to continue his sea-going, he stayed in London, Hull, Cardiff, Liverpool, Sheffield and then finally retired in Liverpool. Saeed was tall, sallow-faced and straight of back. He spoke with his hands in a quiet voice and his dark eyes looked right into you.

He was a tremendous help to us with unravelling the problems of the Somali seafarers in Liverpool. They all sailed as Somali crews with the result that they had no need to learn English in order to continue their careers aboard British ships. In retirement this made life very difficult for them. The majority had joined British vessels in war-time. Because they were cheap and efficient labour, the companies kept them on after the war with the result that Liverpool became their home. Saeed guided many to us and, on every visit, he was accompanied by three or four of his compatriots.

There had been a Somali Centre in Princes Avenue in one of the ground floor rooms of a completely dilapidated building. A small grant, which the City Fathers afforded them, was stopped for a while and the Centre closed. Saeed opened his home to them and fought their cause. As a result, when I retired a new Somali Centre was being built in Granby Street. This was essential because, whilst their children's children have been able to integrate, the older folk need a sanctuary. There will be no more seafarers needed today.

There are always favourites. Of them all, Ronnie comes out on top. I could hardly forget the day we first met. We were in the middle of a party wishing "bon voyage" to one of the Chaplains, Philip Jones,, who was leaving Liverpool to become the Missions to Seamen Chaplain in Colombo. Philip had been staying with us as he waited for the posting to be confirmed. I never did take him to the airport.

"Padre, please go to the Promenade Hospital in Southport. There's an Asian seaman in the Intensive Care Unit. It's urgent."

That was how I came to meet Ronnie Coutinho.

Ronnie, an Indian citizen, was the Third Officer on the Saudi-flag "Macca", when she docked in Liverpool in July 1983. The ship was unloading a cargo of rice-bran, when on the 19th July, during his cargo watch, Ronnie was struck by the grab of the discharging crane. The injuries to his lower body were critical. He was rushed to the Royal Hospital in Liverpool. They could not help. The ambulance speeded the twenty-five miles to the Spinal Injuries Unit in Southport. I called it the "miracle unit" and, when I first met Ronnie, a miracle was needed.

He was alive. The medical team declared that he was in a critical condition and was not optimistic, but Ronnie did not die. It was typical of the Liverpool dockers to organise a collection of monies, which enabled the father to travel from Bombay and stay in an hotel in Southport for a number of weeks.

The progress was slow and, without doubt, Ronnie passed through the "valley of the shadow". That he did emerge was because of his courage, the skill and love of the medical care and, I believe, the mantle of prayer with which we surrounded them all.

Many weeks were to pass before the "responsibility of liability" was accepted. The final settlement was to take six years. We were all involved in the battle with the Home Office about his status in this country and eventually permission was granted for him to stay "until his medical treatment is completed". Ronnie knew full well that his treatment would never come to an end. The consultant's report made that quite clear. "Due to paralysis, this man is severely disabled and will be confined to a wheel chair for the rest of his life." Ronnie has no movement from below his waist. Back in Bombay, his mother suffers Parkinson's disease, his father has a heart condition and they both live on the fourth floor of a building with no lift. Obviously Ronnie cannot return to his home.

I discovered that as soon as money was available, Ronnie was sending most of it to support his younger brother, who was studying for the law in America. In India most families support each other in this way.

Ronnie is a Roman Catholic and with the support of the Church in Southport and help from us, he joined a group for a visit to Lourdes. To the hilarity of everyone, he returned home with a broken arm! He had fallen out of his chair.

He is undergoing experiments with computer controlled braces, which should allow him to walk in a limited fashion. We drove him to London for the fitting.

The real story of Ronnie is not about his medical condition or survival. He is still under thirty, bright eyed, intelligent and keen to make a new start in life. He bought a car and slings his wheel chair out, fixes the wheels and heaves himself into it with a broad grin and merry quip. He frequently came to the Mission and there was hardly a ship we visited without a query about Ronnie. We all loved him. He takes a computer course at College. He raises money for the disabled, enough to purchase a mini-bus in Southport. The story of Ronnie is all about rebirth ... a new vibrant personality had emerged.

These are some of the people whom I shall never forget.

15.

Presidente Jose Pardo

The plight of the Peruvian vessel Presidente Jose Pardo touched the hearts and, in many cases, the lives of the Liverpool folk and certainly coloured our work in the Mission for sixteen months. The story deserves to be told in full and is put together by Juan Gammara Nevado, who was the Union representative aboard. The full statement was dated 25th March 1988. We helped Juan to put it together.

"The Peruvian freighter M/V Presidente Jose Pardo at present impounded in Bootle docks is owned by the Compania Peruana de Vapores (CPV) ... a State-controlled Company with an efficient Management. (sic)

"The following statement intends to convey the men's frustration with the inefficient management and is in no way meant to be disrespectful to the Captain or any of the Officers of the ship.

Background

"The ship left Callao (Peru) on the 15th September 1987, loaded cargo at Chilean and Peruvian ports before proceeding to the Panama Canal. The ship was impounded there for five days due to an alleged non-payment of debts incurred by other ships belonging to C.P.V. The freighter took on fuel at Cristobal (Panama) and also was held up for three days to await the arrival of an extra engineer to enable the freighter to proceed across the Atlantic to Liverpool.

"On the 30th October, as soon as we had docked, we were aware that the ship was under arrest. We discharged all cargo, including that destined for Bremen (Germany) and Oslo (Norway). This was completed by the 15th November 1987. Since then we have been stranded here with the added communication problems associated with not speaking English.

"Nearly four months now we have been waiting a solution to this impasse caused by alleged debts incurred by ships belonging to C.P.V.

Therefore our claim is:

a) That we are owed two month's additional charter fees from 15th September to 15th November.

b) Travel allowances, agreed by our Union and C.P.V. in 1984; this is a ten dollar allowance for every day a C.P.V ship is in port. Therefore we claim the following days: the five days impounded in Panama, the three days waiting period in Cristobal plus over thirty days outstanding while the ship has been under arrest in Liverpool.

Difficulties compounded

"On the 9th February, the General Secretary of the C.P.V. Seamen's Union based at Callao, Peru, Senor Victor Irala del Castillo informed me that an indefinite general strike had been called aboard all C.P.V. ships as from the 10th February 1988, to complain about pay and conditions in the Company.

"After a meeting of the men aboard the M/V Presidente Jose Pardo we agreed to heed the strike call from our Union and we signed a letter to the Captain informing him of our intention of withdrawing our labour commencing the 10th February 1988.

"Our Union have told us that we have the following grievances against C.P.V.

1. Low Pay

"At present pay is one hundred dollars (£50) per month, agreed in 1988. This sum included all overtime, plus rates and other dues, but every seaman does not ever get this low amount as many do not have the chance to work overtime. Because of this, their wives at home in Peru, with several mouths to feed, are forced to manage on 50 dollars a month (£25), which even in Peru is too low for adequate subsistence for a family.

2. Non-implementation of Peruvian Government policy.

The Peruvian Government has, since July 1986, awarded cost of living rises of 40% and 25% on basic pay, but the Company refuses to pay out despite being ordered to do so by the Courts.

3. Non-payment of school fees

"Every February, when the school year starts, it has been the custom of C.P.V. to lend to its employees the money to pay these essential school fees.

"This year the Company has not kept its promise to do this, causing great concern and anxiety to many seamen with children of school age. We are asking for the usual loan of 200 dollars (£100), which will be repaid over the following ten months.

4. Victimisation of colleagues

"On the 15th February 1988, a 24 hour stoppage was called aboard all the C.P.V. ships in Peruvian ports. Our comrades aboard the M/V Chocono heeded this call and were sacked for it, to be replaced by non-union workers. These strikers, long-standing employees of the Company, were eventually re-instated but had 15 days pay stopped ... all this while berthed in Callao.

5. Harassment by management

"They use any excuse to punish us by stopping days of pay and by accusing us of bringing the good name of Peru into disrepute by continuing the strike.

"We are therefore requesting a guarantee in writing that no reprisals will be taken against any of our members.

6. Repatriation to Home Country

"In accordance with the provisions of Section 19, page 8 of the International Transport Federation (ITF) repatriation to home country after 14 days of a ship being arrested or impounded; this transfer to home port to be at the arrested ship's Company expense.

"The present situation on the Presidente Jose Pardo in particular is this:

"On the 10th February, acting on instructions from our Union Headquarters, we made placards and put them on the side of the ship. We then began to demonstrate peacefully aboard our own vessel. The Chief Officer, Edgar Ortiz Sanchez, then proceeded to tear down our placards and threw them over the side. When we remonstrated with him he exploded into a furious rage and told us, in the presence of the Captain, to complain to whomever we wished, but no advertising would be allowed on <u>his</u> ship!

"After this we proceeded to Colonsay House in Crosby, Liverpool, which is the headquarters of the Mersey Mission to Seamen, who put us in touch with the Peruvian Consul in London, Senor Miguel Pons, who promised to intercede with the Captain for us. Also, we called our Union General Secretary in Callao, Peru, to inform him of the dramatic and unhappy turn of events aboard the Presidente Jose Pardo.

"The above complaint is released to the public with the approval of the Compania Peruana de Vapores Seamen's Union, based in Callao, and also on behalf of all the seamen aboard this ship, who wish to see a peaceful and amicable settlement so that they be reunited with their families in Peru.

"At the heart of this dispute is the style of management of the Presidente of the C.P.V.'s Board of Directors, Senor Juan Manuel Ortaneda, who had failed his promise to improve the pay and conditions of service of the seamen and make the Company viable. Instead, he had led the Company into the mire of economic chaos by filling important administrative posts with highly paid, but incompetent and boorish officials, whose methods and manners of working have led to the detriment of our Country, our Company and our fellow Union Members, whose efforts have (or would have) earned valuable foreign currency for Peru.

"We are subjected to both physical and mental trauma as various C.P.V. ships are impounded around the world; their crews suffering deprivation and hardship are also aware that their loved ones are having to live below the international poverty levels back home and are unable adequately to feed, clothe and house or educate their children, even to Peru's low standards.

"We are grateful to the Mersey Mission to Seamen for their encouragement and pastoral care and also to Jim Hennigan of the International Transport Federation, who has committed his organisation's assistance until a successful conclusion to our action.

"The media publicity had led to generous support from our comrades in other Unions and moral support from Latin Americans living on Merseyside.

"Our struggle continues until Management is willing to negotiate a new pay deal and to discuss the grievances outlined above, regardless of any settlement with C.P.V.'s creditors. The ideal thing would be a complete blacking of all Peruvian imports and exports until the Peruvian Government realises the extent of human suffering its broken election promises are causing to its citizens around the world and meets our demands for a fair deal.

"In conclusion, dear comrades, may I stress that any help your members feel able to give us will be most gratefully received as our resources are dwindling fast.

"On behalf of my Brothers on strike aboard the Presidente Jose Pardo.

Signed.   Juan Gammarra Nevado.

Union Representative."

That memorandum was circulated on Merseyside and tells the story well. For sixteen months the ship sat in the dock with an empty quayside, not another vessel in sight and with very little activity aboard. There was a sense of desolation and hopelessness in the situation and the Mersey Mission was to play an important part in maintaining the morale of the crew.

When the Presidente arrived in Liverpool, there were some thirty men aboard and we did all we could to create a Christmas for them in 1987, little dreaming that we were to be faced with the same problem for Christmas 1988. That first Christmas we took the Bishop of Warrington, Michael Henshall, and an appropriate number of wine bottles for everyone on the ship and we sat together to enjoy a simple lunch with Captain Vargas.

After lunch the whole crew assembled and Bishop Michael gave a short message of goodwill and then presented the Captain with a Bible. I was never to underestimate the value of taking a Bishop into any situation and it was obvious that the ship's company was grateful for his blessing.

The first Easter we took fifteen men to the airport and they returned home to Lima. There was much excess baggage, but it was all paid for by the Admiralty Marshall, whose writs covered the bulkhead outside the Master's day cabin. At one time those writs would have been nailed to the mast! Nine seaman were flown in as replacements. We all thought that the Admiralty Marshall showed great concern for the crew and we were asked a number of times to check formally that all was well.

The frustration was clearly illustrated, when we heard that the wife of the Chief Engineer had been seriously injured in a car accident in Lima. In the Mission, we were able to make contact with the elder son and kept in touch with what was happening. Normally, in this situation, a man would be flown home on compassionate grounds at the expense of the shipping company and with no delay. But, this was not a normal situation and in spite of the endeavours of many people, we failed.

The Company ruling was that the Chief Engineer had to find his own fare home and also pay for his replacement to be flown to the U.K. This was impossible. Our main contribution was to keep in touch with the family at Lima. Eventually, the Chief's wife was removed from Intensive Care and a certain amount of pressure was relieved. The ultimate irony was that, even if the return home had been possible, the Chief was convinced that he would lose his job with the Company.

Aboard the ship was the Captain's nephew, Ernesto, aged eighteen. He had joined for a three month's holiday! It became a very extended break. On arrival he spoke hardly any English and, when he left we assured him that his English was still deplorable, but his command of Scouse was perfect. We explained that Jimmy Tarbuck's definition of Scouse was that it was a mixture of Irish and Rubbish. I was not certain that he understood our message, as he surrounded himself with laughter. Ernesto was to spend many hours helping in the Mission and we all enjoyed his company. His ambition was to join the Police in Lima and I know that we had furthered his education. In the end, he stayed with us for a year.

A school visit to a Coastline ship. "Thankyou Captain Morrison!"

Seafarers love children. The ship's company asked if they could give a party aboard and we arranged for a group of youngsters from a local Special School to be taken aboard. They understood that these children needed special care and the party was a great success with the result that groups of men attended the School to help with sport. At the end of term, I took a number of the crew and I presented a photograph of the ship's party with formal speeches, much clapping and a good sing-song.

We were all proud of the fact that not one night of the whole sixteen months did the Mission mini-bus fail to turn up at the bottom of the gangway about seven o'clock to bring the men into Colonsay House. Maintaining the morale for the whole ship's company was our main task and I believe that we achieved it. One night we arrived in time to attach a rope to the bus in order to drag the gangway away from the quayside into which it was about to tumble. There were no shore-gangs available for the Presidente, just an empty dockside.

Football played a firm part of the Mission's life-style and the team off the Presidente was formidable. We arranged many matches. During this time we had accepted responsibility for the social and sight-seeing life of a dozen Mexican cadets, who were in Liverpool with "Blue Funnel" for an induction course prior to their first trip to sea. We fixed a six week programme and those Mexicans proved to be naturals for many a game of football with the Peruvians.

Plesseys were excellent in their care for the ship, not only arranging football, but providing social evenings to help the men relax and enjoy Merseyside.

The Port Police team was always ready to tackle any ship and the Peruvians finally overcame their shock in finding our only police woman, Maureen, in goal. She was fearless in flattening any of the opposition intent on scoring goals. I was not sure who enjoyed it most!

One surprise was a telephone call from the Roman Catholic Archbishop's office asking that I organised a visit to the ship for a South American Bishop. I carefully inquired as to why they had not used their own Stella Maris chaplain and was told that their man rarely called on the Presidente.

They all finally went home early in 1989. With the help of the Swedish and Norwegian chaplains, we took them to the airport, There was no doubt that Liverpool had done its stuff. The ship left behind many friends and most people on Merseyside were able to roll off their tongues the name Presidente Jose Pardo with a good Peruvian accent. Once the crew had departed, the vessel was quickly sold to the China Steam Navigation Company and the name Presidente Jose Pardo was no more.

Sadly, it is not unusual for ships to be laid up these days like dockside graveyards. In Birkenhead, we had four elegant Cunarders sitting alongside each other, empty and derelict. A picture of them appeared in the Liverpool Echo, producing groans from Merseysiders bewailing past glories. A short distance away was a far sadder story.

Into Birkenhead had come the Ghanaian ship, Micene, with fourteen men aboard. The smelly cargo of cattle feed was off-loaded. The Dutch Captain and the Chief Engineer both departed home, leaving the Ghanaians to their own devices.

In charge was the Mate, William, together with his wife, Susie. The owner was in financial trouble and the Ghanaians had received no pay for a number of months. So they remained aboard, because a seafarer cannot just walk off a ship in a strange country and these men had no money to take them home. They were trapped and just stayed with the hope that something would happen to resolve their dilemma.

The future of such men is determined by faceless people with whom they cannot communicate. They stayed because there was no other place for them. If the vessel could have been sold, the first charge would have been to pay the crew, but the ship was very old and there on the other side of the wharf sat the four eight year old Cunarders. There was little hope for the Ghanaians.

We took aboard some warm clothing as the weather was getting colder. There was little work for the men aboard the ship, so we gave them card games and board games and books and jig-saws and magazines. They had no television until we gave them one. They had no money. Each day we collected them and brought them through the tunnel to the Mission. Then there were trips into the country, because seafarers never see green fields and smell the grass. Russell, our Welfare man, did much of the work, kept their book-cases full and became a friend.

We worked along with Peter McGrath, the British Sailors' Society' Chaplain. Our relationship with Peter was tremendous, keeping each other informed and just getting on with the work. There was only one solution for the Ghanaians. We involved the Press and the local television companies and, above all, the local M.P., Frank Field, who proved to be a tower of strength.

At last the men were able to return home, with partial pay and free air tickets. Naturally, a few weeks later, the ship was sold ... too late for the ship's company! They had won nothing ... apart from our love and care and blessing. Oddly enough, my memory of them is of smiling faces, great companionship and Susie, large in a bright floral dress, mother to them all. Memory need not be sad.

At the same time as Micene was sitting idle in Birkenhead, on our side of the Mersey, there was the River Rima, Nigerian National Line, well into the sixth month of her arrest. And just up the dock system, we had a Yugoslav and an Italian vessel, both with writs "on their masts". No wonder I thought that the lot of the seafarer had been turned back a hundred years and that our work in the docks was as necessary as when we started in 1856!

My last thought is of a real friend, Gupta, an Indian Second Engineer. His ship had been stranded in Birkenhead for six months. The vessel was owned by Mitsubishi of Japan, where we all thought no-one was bankrupt! We took the crew to a Liverpool Travel Agent to arrange the return home. Next day they departed for Heathrow with baggage and three refrigerators. We never did hear how that aircraft became airborne, but it must have, because Gupta was to remain a regular correspondent.

All these stories could be told endlessly and, in them all, the theme is the same ... the seafarer comes last!

16.

The Good Shepherd

When I was asked by the Bishop to return to the Mission in 1979 after just five years as Vicar of Rainhill, one of my sadnesses was to discover that a beautiful wood carving had been stolen from our Chapel of the Good Shepherd. At the end of the war, a seafarer, who had survived the Battle of the Atlantic even though two ships had been torpedoed under him, had presented the carving as an act of thanksgiving on behalf of all those who had come safely through the perils of the war at sea.

Most people give memorials for the dead, often in an attempt to prolong the memory, but this anonymous donor was just grateful for being alive. The wooden plaque had been bought in 1950 at Oberammergau and depicted the Wise Men presenting their respective gifts to the Infant Jesus. It was placed on the wall behind my prayer desk and I had grown accustomed to touch it each day to remind me that the day was to be given to God. The person, who stole it, could not have understood what it meant to me.

I approved of the title "Chapel of the Good Shepherd" as it reminded me that the shepherds in the days of Jesus always walked in front of their flock, so that the sheep could follow in safe foot-steps. That is what Jesus meant when He called Himself the Good Shepherd. In the West we are daft enough to drive sheep from behind with dogs and whistles and sticks!

Although the present Chapel at Colonsay House in Crosby is much smaller than the previous Chapel of the Good Shepherd in Kingston House at Pier Head, we were able to take with us many of the "good things".

On the wall is a brass plate in memory of Fell of Frisco with the quotation from 1 Cor. 16.13., "Quit you like men, be strong." Alongside hangs the board with the names of all the Chaplains, starting with the Reverend Bellamy and followed by all his successors. My name is there twice, 1962 - 1974 and 1979 - 1989. The wags in the Diocese referred to my last ten years as the "second coming".

The Font is in memory of William Burnaby Southouse Star, R.D., Master Mariner. The Bishop's Chair and the Hymn Board were presented in memory of Charles William Banbury, Master Mariner and Marine Superintendent of Clan Line and long serving member of the Mission's Committee. A magnificent Flying Angel kneeler was designed and worked by his wife, Dilys. Both Charles and Dilys have now passed on, but remain in memory as the greatest of friends and bundles of fun. Dilys's cream meringues were a legend in our family!

All these gifts and so much more mark the love and gratitude that friends showed to the Mission and all that it stood for in their lives. That love helped create the atmosphere needed by our visiting seafarers as they "popped in" for some moments of prayer.

There was one occasion when I found a man walking and gazing in the Chapel and we fell into conversation. He was an ex-serviceman and, when I pursued his war career, he said that he had been a "chippy" in the Royal Navy. We talked of ships and he dropped the name Folkestone. I pointed to the ship's crests on the Chapel wall. There was H.M.S. Folkestone. His face lit up as he fondly fingered the wood and traced the patterns. "I carved this!" We sat and chatted. As he left the Chapel, I reminded him that after we had both departed this world, his crest would remain to remind the world of lives lost, battles won and the simple craft that he had shared with the Carpenter of Nazareth. He looked as though I had given him gold!

Let the inscription in the Chapel tell the story.

"The ship's crests, which adorn these walls originally formed part of the furnishings of the Flotilla Chapel, Gladstone Dock, Liverpool, during the Second World War, 1939 - 1945. With many others they there recalled, day by day, the service at sea of the ships in the Escort Groups of the Western Approaches Command, whose names they bore.

With the disbandment of the command at the end of the war the Crests of the undermentioned ships were given for safe keeping to the Mersey Mission to Seamen to be placed in the Chapel of the Good Shepherd.

H.M.S. Vanoc	H.M.S. Deptford
H.M.S. Viscount	H.M.S. Folkestone
H.M.S. Walker	H.M.S. Hesperus
H.M.S. Winchelsea	H.M.S. Leith
H.M.S. Witch	H.M.S. Wellington
H.M.S. Richmond	H.M.S. Wanderer
H.M.S. Pegasus	H.M.S. Ramsey

HISTORICAL NOTES.

In March, 1941, the U-boats, commanded by the three German "Ace" Captains were all sunk by the ships of the Western Approaches Command:

U-47 (Prien)	Sunk by H.M.S. Wolverine.
U-99 (Kretschmer)	Sunk by H.M.S. Walker.
U-99 (Schepke)	Sunk by H.M.S. Vanoc.

"On the 9th of July, 1944, the Royal Navy and the nation sustained a great loss in the death of Captain Frederick John Walker, C.B., D.S.O.***, R.N., who died in Liverpool after playing a leading part in the invasion of France. He was one of the most inspiring figures of the anti-submarine war. His ship, or the Escort Group he commanded, destroyed twenty U-boats".

COMMANDERS-IN-CHIEF, WESTERN APPROACHES

1939-1943 Admiral Sir Martin Dunbar-Naismith, V.C.,K.C.B.

(Plymouth)

1941-1943 Admiral Sir Percy Noble, K.C.B., C.V.O.

(Liverpool)

1943-1945 Admiral Sir Max Horton, G.C.B., D.S.O.

(Liverpool)

This inscription tells the bare facts and is a reminder of the Flotilla Club long gone from Gladstone Dock. All that did remain when I arrived on the scene in 1961 was a plaque on the wall on the quayside. When the shed was destroyed, I assumed that it found its way to the Maritime Museum.

Over the years, I have spoken to many men who used both the Flotilla Club and its Chapel. One old matelot put it this way.

"Many of us slipped in for a quiet word before we sailed out into the Atlantic, but when we returned safely we headed for home."

That was an honest man! He went on to talk about padres in the Club.

"Any guy who ventured into the Chapel was given a Prayer Card."

To my surprise, he was back in a few days and he presented to me the card given him by the padre some forty-five years before. It is now framed and hangs alongside the Crests, which came from the Flotilla Club's Chapel. If you look carefully at the card, you will see the interior of the Chapel and the Crests fixed to a beam above the altar. These are the words on that Prayer Card.

˙THE FLOTILLA CHAPEL
LIVERPOOL

"When thou passest through the waters, I will be with thee."

Isaiah 43,v.2.

"Almighty God, Bless and guard my loved ones at home and all amongst whom I live and work. Open my eyes to know Thy will at all times and guide and strengthen me to fulfil it. All this I ask in the name of Jesus Christ, My Lord and Saviour. Amen."

That chance meeting was a timely reminder that I should never under-estimate any contact with a seafarer, as the most unlikely character might turn out to be the one with whom I had really communicated .

Canon Bill Evans, self, Archdeacon Eric Evans
We covered fifty years in the Mission

I much enjoyed moments playing the organ, which was presented to the Mission in memory of an old golfing friend, Les Davies. It had been my pleasure to marry Erlys and Les just as few years earlier in a Swansea Church. They had a brief, but happy few years before Les was to die. Les's golf was as rotten as mine, but we talked well as we hacked our way around the course. Friendship goes on.

So much in the Chapel of the Good Shepherd was part of the story of Liverpool and the Battle of the Atlantic. A good example is the inscription alongside the altar, written by one of my predecessors, Canon G. W. Evans.

"This altar-piece was originally executed for the Chapel of the Naval Base at Aultbea which, during the years 1939-1945 served Loch Ewe, simultaneously established as a routing port for the North Atlantic convoys. At the end of the war, by reason of its obvious appropriateness and through the kindness of a friend based in Aultbea, it came by permission of the Chaplain of the Fleet into our possession. It was conceived, designed and painted by Lieutenant J.S.Marshall, R.N.V.R., and its history is best told in the artist's own words:

"When the first Chaplain came to Aultbea he converted a store hut into what is now the Chapel. He asked me to assist him in preparing a drawing for an altar-piece which could easily be produced with the means at our disposal. This I did and also offered to paint the decorative panel myself. We acquired the necessary wood in the Base, but had to beg the paint from Merchant ships. Five very crude colours only were available, the Base at that time not being advanced enough to boast a paint store. The paint was most unsuitable and I often despaired of the whole project. Eventually the painting was finished and the joiner was called in to make the frame. I don't remember his name, but he made a splendid job of it. The crown on top, although strictly known as a Naval Crown, is more frequently used by the Merchant Service. It was carved by a pattern-maker after I had made him the drawings on the wood. I think his name was Trigg, but whether or not, he did a delightful piece of work. The text and subjects were chosen by the Chaplain, and as well as embracing the Base, the panel also includes the Merchant Navy, Naval Escort Vessels and Boom Defence personnel. It depicts a convoy of Merchant Ships entering harbour after an ocean crossing. If I remember rightly one of the ships from which we begged paint was a hospital ship since lost during the invasion of Italy."

It has been set up here to form the Reredos of this, "The Altar of the Western Approaches", where it will remain a treasured and sacred possession."

G.W.Evans

Chaplain Superintendent.

When I received a letter out of the blue from J.S.Marshall, he was a voice from the past. He asked whether we had retained the Altar of the Western Approaches when we moved the Mission into Colonsay House in Crosby. I was delighted to respond that his reredos was in good order, and that the words above his painting were as relevant today, as when he first wrote them.

"So He bringeth them unto the haven where they would be."

G.W.Evans, M.B.E.,A.K.C., Honorary Canon in Liverpool Cathedral was Chaplain Superintendent from 1935 to 1957. Not only did he guide the Mission through the Second World War, he completed the first stage of Kingston House in James Street. He moved "good things" from the Chapel in Hanover Street to James Street and, in turn, I moved them to Colonsay House. I noted that my successor promptly separated the reredos from the altar. It is a good alteration, but I trust that the reredos will always remain in the Chapel.

During my years at the Mission, I served happily under three Chairmen, Donald Crawford, Dick Hodges and David Lowry. Each one had great strength and there is no doubt that without their guidance, the Mission would not have weathered the changes and challenges of the Port of Liverpool. I firmly believe that without the encouragement and confidence of the Chairmen and the Committee Members, the Mersey Mission would have sunk without trace along with many other "good things" on Merseyside.

I was pleased that we were able to save the stained glass windows from the Chapel in Kingston House and that we could take them with us to Crosby. Almost my last task before leaving the Mission at Colonsay was to dedicate a window, which incorporated two panels from the Chapel in Kingston House ... two men were remembered, one died in 1942 and the other in 1988. Those who come after us will see a lovely window and I hope they will understand that it was placed there with love. The simple inscription ends with the words, "May the sea bear them kindly", and with them go, our prayers for the family, Lily and Ron and Joyce and Graham. Here is their story.

No-one could have foreseen the huge explosion on the night of 6th July 1988, which ripped apart the oldest, biggest and most profitable oil platform in the North Sea, Piper Alpha. Inside three hours, one hundred and sixty -seven men were dead and the 35,000 ton platform was destroyed. One of the dead was Raymond Leslie Price, whose family, Joyce, his wife, and Graham, his son, were lifelong friends of the Mission.

It was night on Piper Alpha with the quiet hum of pumps drawing off oil and gas from the seabed via 36 underwater wells. Each day they removed 317,000 barrels of oil worth £3.5 million. Most of the 226 crew were off duty after a tough twelve hour shift, only about fifty were working.

At 10 p.m. there was a noise like a banshee as gas escaped under pressure and then a violent blast rocked Piper Alpha. Explosion followed explosion as oil and gas lines ruptured. The lights went out and the workshop roof collapsed. At 10.02 British Telecom's maritime radio station at Wick picked up a report of fire in Piper Alpha's radio room and then the desperate message: "We're abandoning the rig ... We've got to get out of here!" At 10.22

came the worst blast and Piper Alpha was engulfed by a fireball.

The biggest rescue operation ever mounted in the North Sea was under way. Six vessels in the immediate area had responded to the Mayday call. Military and civilian helicopters converged, but it was at least an hour's flying from the mainland. The platform's three support ships scoured the sea for survivors. In the end, Piper Alpha was marked by a huge pall of smoke out of which spouted fire, fed by fountains of escaping gas and oil. At 6.30 p.m., eighteen hours into the rescue operation, it was called off. The final toll was 167 dead.

Over 30,000 men work on 170 offshore installations in the North Sea and over twenty five years more than 300 have died. Removing coal from underground is obviously dangerous, but we must not take oil and gas for granted as they, too, are hard won. As Tom O'Neil, both church counsellor and oil safety manager, put it while paying tribute to those "men of brawn and courage" during the Memorial Service in Aberdeen: "When you cook your dinner today, turn on the engine of your car, or switch on the central heating - say a little prayer."

On the 25th July 1989, in the Chapel of the Good Shepherd at Colonsay House, I dedicated the window in memory of Raymond Leslie Price, off Piper Alpha, and also in memory of Herbert Wilkinson, his father-in-law, who was lost at sea forty six years earlier in the R.M.S. Nova Scotia.

On September 17th, 1942, the German submarine U-177 sailed from Kiel on a fateful mission. Her commander was Kapitan-leutnant Robert Gysae, aged 31, a cold, relentless and dedicated officer. His orders were to take his submarine round the Cape of Good Hope into the hitherto safe waters of the Indian Ocean. By the morning of November 28th, U-177 was off Durban, when soon after sunrise Gysae spotted a speck on the horizon.

Two weeks earlier, the elderly Furness Withy freighter, Nova Scotia, lay at anchor in the little harbour of Massawa in Eritrea. The vessel was built in 1926 and was very small, just 6,796 tons.

She was to carry Italian prisoners of war to Durban to help relieve the labour shortage in South Africa. She sailed on November 14th, crowded with Italians prisoners and civilian internees, almost a thousand.

At 9.12 on that sunny morning, the Nova Scotia had closed to within 1,000 feet of U-177. The three bow torpedo tubes fired.

Three violent explosions shook the ship, oil bunkers caught fire and the bridge was engulfed with flames. There was total confusion. Men were afraid to jump, whilst others fought to reach the rail. Many were burnt and in great pain. Lifeboats on the port side were smashed. The stern reared out of the sea and in six minutes the Nova Scotia disappeared under the ocean. One lifeboat had been launched and was filled with water.

When U-177 surfaced, Gysae heard the cries of "Il Duce! Italia!". The Captain realised what he had done ... torpedoed a vessel full of allies! He called out, "I'm terribly sorry. I will radio Berlin and help will be sent. Be brave."

As they were too close to land and aircraft could have found them, Gysae cruised for an hour and then radioed Berlin.

Hundreds died in a few minutes. Some struggled on until they were exhausted. Others choked to death in the oil. After just an hour, that horror was over, for the rest it was just the beginning.

Men clung to driftwood ... then there would be a scream ... a man disappeared. The sharks had arrived. Death came with horror.

The night came and passed. That Sunday the sun blazed down on the survivors. Then came another night. Ships lamps were seen, but not one vessel stopped to help.

The radio message from U-177 had been received in Berlin, forwarded in code to the German Embassy in Madrid and then on to Lisbon. Portugal was neutral and help was requested because Mozambique was Portuguese and thought to be nearest to Nova Scotia.

The Portuguese training ship Afonso de Albuquerque, a 1,400 ton frigate, was in Lourenco Marques and was ready to sail. Twelve hours after the sinking, the message was received in the frigate. "Proceed immediately full speed to pick up survivors sunk 9 am today." The details were then given placing the Nova Scotia about 180 miles south of Lourenco Marques. The Albuquerque sailed at 2.30 am on the Sunday and arrived in the search area at 6 am. The first survivors were spotted at 1.12 p.m. on the Sunday.

A raft was found with eighteen exhausted men and by the Sunday evening 122 men were saved. Darkness fell and by search-light another six were rescued. By 4 p.m. on the Monday, 183 survivors were aboard and, as a storm was brewing, the search was abandoned to take the sick to port. The rescue vessel arrived into Lourenco Marques at 10 am on the Tuesday.

Only 14 of the Nova Scotia's crew were saved out of the total of 114. Herbert Wilkinson sadly was not amongst them. Nine hundred Italians were lost. All this information was not released in detail until 1965.

The windows will remain in the Chapel of the Good Shepherd and I trust that the stories of the Piper Alpha and the Nova Scotia will not be forgotten.

Another final task before I retired was to take a cheque on behalf of the Shipwrecked Mariners' Society worth sixty pounds to a pensioner in Mulgrave Street in Toxteth ... my "beat" for so many years. He was old and bent and spotless. His one-bed flat was squared-off, ship-shaped and shining. He twinkled a welcome. The flatlet was owned by the Liverpool Housing Trust and the "ancient mariner" was obviously warm and contented with his final berth. There were no problems. With a smile I passed the cheque to him.

"Thank God", he said.

"It's been a pleasure to help you." The twinkle was back.

"You speak for God?"

We both enjoyed the joke. But, as I departed, I rather hoped that his response had been a statement and not a question.

There was one Indian ship where the cabin quickly filled with seamen and I was intrigued by a wood carving on the bulkhead above the desk. It seemed to be just incomprehensible squiggles. After we had all settled, I asked about it and it proved a real can opener.

"It's an old Hindu saying."

They all discussed the translation and to my surprise I realised that I had met the words somewhere before, but could not recall where. At last, they settled on the correct text.

"Lord, make me master of myself,

that I might be a servant of others."

Then, they all turned to me for my explanation. It was a perfect opportunity and I believe that I made full use of it.

I accepted that the saying was appropriate to many religions and that for all of us it posed the problem of how to achieve inner spiritual discipline. They all nodded assent and asked for me to continue.

I suggested that the answer was "prayer", which is common to all the world religions. They again agreed, but moved sharply to the next question.

"Can you tell us how you Christians pray?"

I told them that the disciples had asked Jesus that very question and His answer had been to give us what we now call "The Lord's Prayer". I took them through it phrase by phrase.

Once again, I realised that whenever I was able to talk in depth about personal spirituality, we all seemed to be on the same wave-length. Of course, we come in at different angles on any question, but I always knew that we were spiritual brothers.

Maybe we are all missing the obvious as we rush madly towards the end of the century.

All men cry.

When I bleed, my blood is the same as yours.

All men are hungry, so I can understand

The hunger of the Ethiopian child,

The starving of the world.

I must understand.

 My sorrow is the same pain

As your sorrow's pain.

We are the same.

So how can my God

And your God

Not be the same God?

17.

We will Remember

For almost twenty years, I served as Chaplain in the Royal Naval Reserves, a cultural shock for a man who had been a pilot in the Royal Air Force. We held our weekly drills in H.M.S. Eaglet, which was a "floating hulk" in the South Docks and well known to many thousands of seafarers. When I joined, the Roman Catholic Chaplain was Dick Firth and his full time job was to be prison Chaplain at Walton. He was followed by John White. He started the Stella Maris in Bootle and we became good friends over the years together.

The first task for the Chaplain on Drill Night was to conduct the prayers at Divisions. The full ship's company assembled for the Captain's Inspection. Everyone lined up on the drill deck with much shouting and shuffling and saluting. Then would come the order, "Off caps". This was my cue to step forward for my two minutes of stardom. It really was a challenge. I became, in time, quite expert at lifting pertinent pieces from Thomas a Kempis's "The Imitation of Christ" or that night's Liverpool Echo. Very quickly I discovered that as I walked the decks after Divisions, the old leg was pulled and the topic was dissected. They had listened!

Sadly Eaglet was falling apart and occasionally the lights would flicker and dim. On those nights I invariably ended my "spot" with the Evensong Collect, "Lighten our darkness we beseech Thee, O Lord ... " and this always resulted in a fervent "Amen".

Perhaps the real joy of the Reserves was the fact that these men and women were all volunteers, who gave of their own time for training and were drawn from every facet of possible shore-side occupation. We had a common bond with the Navy and I felt that it was good to meet visiting Naval Ships and be accepted as "one of them". Rarely does a dog collar get such an opportunity and I was proud to be part of such a family. It seemed to open doors wherever I travelled.

My first RNR Commanding Officer -
Captain Harold Duffy

Nothing quite matches the Annual Battle of Atlantic Service in Liverpool Cathedral. Every seat was taken and the music and the trumpets sent shivers down my spine.

> We will remember them.
>
> At the going down of the sun, and in the morning
>
> We will remember them.
>
> They shall grow not old, as we that are left grow old

Age shall not weary them, nor the years condemn.
At the going down of the sun, and in the morning,
We will remember them.

Over the years, the nature of the Service has changed into a Thanksgiving Service for the Seafarer, but it will always retain the element of remembrance of those who gave their lives in that horrendous struggle for survival in the Atlantic. The Service is no longer aimed at "the old and the bold", yet we are still an Island and the sea relentlessly takes its toll.

It was at sunset on August 15th 1945 that Admiral Sir Max Horton, K.C.B.,D.S.O., Commander-in-Chief , Western Approaches, struck his flag and the saga of the Western Approaches passed into history. He had taken over as Commander-in-Chief on November 17th 1942 from Admiral Sir Percy Noble, G.B.E.,K.C.B.,C.V.O.

On August 9th 1945, there was Service of Thanksgiving in our Cathedral and Admiral Horton and Admiral Noble took part. These were the parting words of Admiral Horton.

"Hold your heads high by virtue of the double qualification that having served in the Navy and that of having taken part in the Battle of the Atlantic. Goodbye. Thank you. The very best of luck to you all."

Those were very ordinary words at the end of a battle, which was waged every day of the war without respite. On the very night before the German surrender, three ships were sunk on our doorstep ... two merchant vessels in the Firth of Forth and a mine sweeper in Lyme Bay. Churchill put it this way.

"The one campaign of the Second World War that lasted from the first day to the last. That continuous battle against U-boats and their ultimate defeat was the dominating factor all through the War."

The campaign was directed from Derby House in Liverpool. 2,452 ships were lost in the Atlantic. The British Merchant Navy lost 30,248 men. The Royal Navy lost 73,642 men, most of them in the Atlantic, where submarines sank 175 warships. The Germans built 1,162 submarines ... they lost 784. Statistics numb the mind, the reality was worse.

No-one could ever forget his first encounter with Admiral Stephenson, nicknamed "Monkey Stephenson". At the outbreak of the war, the Admiral was recalled from retirement, even though he was over seventy years of age. He was sent to Tobermory on the West coast of Scotland.

Here the various Groups did their final warm-ups before tackling the North Atlantic, the convoys and hunting packs of U-boats. As the majority of each ship's company was "hostilities only", they had to be given a quick, sharp shock, if they were to survive. Trades had to be mastered in weeks and months, not in years as in the peace-time Navy. Monkey Stephenson was the man chosen to put the fear of God into the final training at Tobermory.

A story, which probably has gone the rounds as long as there have been Navies, has also been attributed to him. He would board a ship unannounced, at an impossible hour, and create havoc. The legendary story is that on one such occasion, Monkey placed his cap on the deck and indicated to a passing matelot, "That's a bomb!" Naturally, the quick thinking lad promptly booted it over the side. The Admiral did not flinch, announced "Man overboard!" and started his stop-watch.

The first time that I met Admiral Stephenson was in May 1962 at the back-end of the Cathedral, as we assembled with all the top-brass for the Battle of Atlantic Service. There he stood, five feet tall with his ceremonial sword tucked in like a crutch, as it almost dragged the ground. He came towards me.

"Who are you?"

"Evans, sir, the Mersey Mission to Seamen."

That did not seem to impress him one little bit. He gave a sort of a grunt.

"Are you any good?"

I knew that this was the moment which had faced many a young officer in Tobermory. If I showed humility, he would have kicked me over the side. I was amazed to hear my instinctive reply to his challenge.

"Yes, sir, I'm the right man for the job!"

"Quite right, my boy, shouldn't do it, if you weren't!"

No wonder decades before, the men were pleased to escape to the North Atlantic storms and the U-boats. He smiled, gave a nod of approval and stumped off to his place in the procession. This was the "Terror of Tobermory", then in his nineties!

A few years later, the old Eaglet was towed away for scrap and lay beached on the mud off Garston. That really was the end of an era. A new "concrete frigate", two storeys and all glass, was commissioned at Trafalgar Dock by Admiral Stephenson. The ship's company marched proudly through the City from the Cathedral, where during the Service I had read the Dedication Prayer for the new Eaglet. Back at the new headquarters, on the edge of the Mersey, we all lined up on the quayside. Monkey mounted the dais, so we might see him, and switched off the bank of microphones and told us to "break ranks" and come about him. In simple language, he told us who we were and what we should do and how to achieve it. His voice cleared the Mersey and I am certain that the dockers in Birkenhead thought that he was getting at them!

"Johnnie Walker" is a well known name on Merseyside. It was my privilege on many occasions to attend the Annual Dinner and on the next morning conduct the Memorial Service at the Bootle War Memorial for the "Walker's Old Boys".

This was the late Captain Frederick John Walker, R.N., Companion of the Order of the Bath and holder of the D.S.O. and three Bars. The Admiralty issued a communiqué in 1950, five and a half years after his death, listing the Navy's greatest achievements and it included this tribute to Captain Walker.

"Captain Walker, more than any other, won the Battle of the Atlantic. His methods had amazing success and more than any other factor gave the Royal Navy supremacy. It is only now that we have learned the full impact he had on the enemy. No tribute could be too high for the work he carried out.

This ace killer of submarines not only showed what mastery in this art could do, but by his example, infected all those others concerned with him in this business with the same enthusiasm.

His death was directly attributable to the overstrain which he suffered in setting that admirable example."

His body rested in the Flotilla Chapel in Gladstone Dock before the Service in the Cathedral. Then, on a gun carriage, the body was taken through the streets with hundreds of sailors and Wrens behind. Finally, placed aboard the destroyer Hesperus, and making way between an incoming convoy out beyond the Bar Lightship, this great man was laid to rest. All of this is part of the story of Liverpool and even though time is fast running out for Walker's Old Boys, I was proud to be used and accepted by them.

During one fortnight with the Royal Navy, I was sent as "acting Chaplain" to the Gunnery School in H.M.S. Excellent. Visiting other ships, I discovered a real treasure, hidden and unused, in the stores in H.M.S. Vernon. It was the Chalice and Paten, which the ship's company of Starling had presented for use aboard their vessel in memory of Captain Walker. I hoped that they might have been returned to Bootle for safe-keeping, but failed in my time in the Reserves to achieve it.

When I came to Liverpool, I was intrigued by the Merchant Navy Memorial at Pier Head and was amazed that on my first Remembrance Sunday on Merseyside, it was totally ignored. I felt that I had to do something about it!

To be correct, the Memorial is not specifically for the Merchant Navy. Not all merchant seamen actually served on merchant ships. Some were "press-ganged" under the "T.124X Agreement" to provide deck and engine-room personnel to handle the mercantile-type machinery, which was fitted into new ships. The Memorial marks those who died under such an Agreement. We all called it the Merchant Navy Memorial, even though all the named had sailed under the White Ensign.

I wrote a letter to the Liverpool Echo, merely stating that I would be taking prayers at twelve noon on Remembrance Sunday at Pier Head for the Merchant Navy. The main parade at St. George's Plateau was over by eleven-thirty that morning, so I toddled down to the Memorial and waited.

To my astonishment, when I arrived at Pier Head, I found a dozen Bunny Girls, complete with fuzz on their sterns and tassels on the upper deck. They were a brave sight. I tactfully inquired and discovered that it was a publicity exercise for a night club. I could not help but notice that these bunnies were getting a bit blue as the wind whipped up the Mersey. I was like the Johnny Walker Whisky advert in my long clerical cloak and all twelve bunnies suggested that they deserved a cuddle!

Five minutes before noon, some fifty men and women arrived from St. George's Plateau, intent on joining my Act of Remembrance. I was not too certain what they made of the set-up, when with a smile I introduced the bunnies as my choir! The girls had asked if they could join in the Service. When almost three decades later, I conducted my final Service at Pier Head with standards and bugles and over one hundred and fifty folk and wreaths were cast upon the water, members of that 1962 effort came forward to remind me of the famous choir.

The Royal Naval Association, Liverpool Branch, had excellent premises at the end of the M62 at Bowring Park. We shared many important occasions there and had great fun. Princess Alice presented me with a Certificate of Thanks from the R.N.A. on one windy day. Those shipmates took every opportunity for a parade or a concert or a celebration.

One beautiful ceremony was the Dedication of their Memorial Stone. It was a granite bollard from the Liverpool Docks and it bore the inscription ...

To the eternal memory of departed shipmates,
in peace and war.
A Tribute to their loyalty and comradeship,
we shall treasure evermore.

A lovely garden was established and it became the focus of all ceremonial thereafter.

It was at the R.N.A. at Bowring Park that I conducted the Inauguration Service for the Liverpool Association of Wrens. The Chairman was Elsie Baring, who served in the Wrens during the War and whose husband had been Fleet Air Arm pilot. The President was Dame Marion Kettlewell, who joined the Wrens as a M.T. Driver in 1941 and retired as Director of the Wrens in 1970. She was an old friend of mine, so the Inauguration went with a swing and a smile. On the 26th November 1917, the First Lord of the Admiralty, Sir Eric Geddes, submitted a letter to his Sovereign, King George V and it started with these remarkable words.

"Sir Eric Geddes, with his humble duty, begs to inform Your Majesty, that the Board of Admiralty have under consideration the possibility of substituting women for men ..."

You must imagine the Scouse comments as I opened my address with that statement.

In 1984, a Memorial Stone had been placed in the American "natural forest" Garden at the Liverpool International Garden Festival. The Stone commemorated the United States Army's Eighth Air Force - the Mighty Eighth - of which more than twenty-six thousand were killed in action. The R.N.A. in Bowring Park had the wisdom and kindness to ask that the Memorial Stone be moved to be placed alongside theirs in the Garden Of Remembrance. It was my privilege to rededicate it in memory of those who gave their lives for freedom.

Kirkby is a vast new town with a population of over seventy thousand. Most of them were moved out of Liverpool, where the planner's answer had been to establish Kirkby and Skelmersdale. I became involved with Kirkby.

For twelve years, I had been the Diocesan Chaplain to the Girls Friendly Society. Dame Marion Kettlewell, when she retired as Director of the Wrens, had become the General Secretary of the G.F.S in London and had asked that I took on the Chairmanship of the Girls at Work Organisation. The G.F.S. placed workers in many areas in the country to keep an eye on the problems which young girls had to face in factories and stores. In most factories, women tend to make up the majority of the work-force. This was how in the Kirkby factories, I found myself involved with organising what G.F.S. called "Life Style Courses". It was the beginning of my contact with Kirkby.

Following a telephone call, I found myself one evening in a pub in the centre of Kirkby surrounded by a group of enthusiasts. The matter under discussion was the forming of a Royal Naval Association in the new town. I was supposed to know all about it! We got on with it, the Club headquarters was built and in spite of my protests I was elected President. When I retired, I tried to resign the presidency, but was promptly made Life President to keep me quiet. They are a great bunch of characters and I am proud to be associated with them.

My annual high-spot in Kirkby is billed as "Battle of Atlantic (Veterans) ... A Service of Remembrance and Thanksgiving." This all started because the folk in charge of the Battle of Atlantic Service in the Cathedral on the first Sunday in every May decided that the R.N.A.'s in the area would not be allowed to carry their standards or march in the parade. As many were actually involved in the Battle of the Atlantic, they rebelled. Kirkby set the pattern by holding their own Service in the afternoon. Most other R.N.A.'s now do the same. So we march through Kirkby from St. Chad's back to the Club with ensigns flying and brass band blowing. Many friendships have been formed over the years and they know how to handle a R.N.R. Chaplain.

A Dog Collar in the Docks

The Falklands War touched us in Liverpool. I believe that about forty Royal Navy Ships were involved, but they required the support of over fifty Merchant vessels. Perhaps the most remarkable sight on our television screens was the Canberra, painted white, sitting in San Carlos Sound. She seemed such an easy target. We knew that ships would be lost. This was war.

On my desk in the Mission were the crew lists of all the Merchant Navy vessels engaged in the conflict and I had marked all the men living in my catchment area. Against those names, I placed the telephone number of their parish priests, so that, if it became necessary, I would be able to make speedy contact for the priests to break news to the next of kin. And, sadly, it happened.

At 0430 hours on 2nd April 1982, one hundred and fifty men of the Argentine Special Forces landed by helicopter at Mullet Creek, which was just three miles from Port Stanley, the capital of the Falkland Islands. By 0930 hours that day, the small garrison had surrendered. War began.

On the 14th April the Atlantic Conveyor, a large container ship owned by Cunard, was laid up in Liverpool. She was just another unwanted vessel. Thirty days later, with twelve of her crew dead, she was at the bottom of the South Atlantic.

In a mere ten days she had been refitted and sailed from Britain as an "Aircraft carrier". On the decks, the containers were stacked four high to act as a shelter and windbreak for the aircraft. As a container ship, she normally would could carry seven hundred twenty foot containers together with nine hundred vehicles on her car decks. With the stern ramp, it was possible to load and unload with great speed. For this journey, there were thousands of tons of stores, food, military equipment and enough tentage for a brigade of soldiers. Of vital importance for the campaign, there were six Wessex and five Chinook helicopters and fourteen Sea and R.A.F. Harriers.

Disaster struck on the 25th May, when the Atlantic Conveyor had almost reached the comparative safety of San Carlos Sound. Two Argentine Super Etenards launched two Exocets as she turned

160

into Falkland Sound. The air raid warning came at 1930 hours and two minutes later the missiles struck.

Within half an hour, the fire was out of control and Captain North ordered "Abandon ship". Twelve men died, including the Captain.

There were six families on Merseyside involved in the tragedy of the Atlantic Conveyor. The telephone call that I received from the Ministry of Defence was merely a request to inform the next of kin that Conveyor had been hit. I protested that such a message was unhelpful and would create unnecessary anguish. The Ministry refused to give any further details. I contacted Cunard. The Company knew that my six seafarers were all safe and that was the message that I passed on to the next of kin. Within twenty minutes, all the parish priests involved telephoned me back to report that the news had been given.

Typically, seafarers and families on Merseyside asked that we would organise a Service at Pier Head. This was done with the full support of the Chaplains of the Apostleship of the Sea and the British Sailors' Society. The Unions handled the publicity, basically by word of mouth. About a thousand people were present, as in a simple Service, we remembered Captain North and all the lives lost. For twenty minutes we made a natural response to tragedy.

Before the ship had left Liverpool, most of the crew had spent their last evening in the nearest pub, the Prince of Wales. Some weeks after the sinking, the Mayor of Sefton, the remarkable Jennie Kemp, took me along to the Prince of Wales, where, after a prayer, she unveiled a painting of the Atlantic Conveyor.

For Jennie this was a traumatic experience, as for many years she worked with the sea-going personnel of Cunard and was known by seafarers all over the world. Jennie probably holds the record of being the first customer in the Prince of Wales who ever ordered a cup of tea ... and got it!

I counted Miss Jennie Kemp and Sir Kenneth Stoddart, our Lord Lieutenant, who opened Colonsay House, as not only great allies of the Mission, but formidable people who understood the purpose of our work. We were lucky to have them.

Miss Jenny Kemp, M.B.E., J.P.
Mayor of Sefton 1983-84, 1988-89.

Many weeks later in our Cathedral, we held a Service to remember those who had lost their lives aboard Atlantic Conveyor and my task was to give the address. All the next of kin were there from all over U.K. and I was proud of the way in which those shattered families displayed their courage.

Cunard had shown me the signals, which had come in from across the world from all their fleet. Captain North had the nick-name of "Captain Birdseye" and was obviously much loved. Seamen invariably find the right words. There was no better thought than that of a man who had first sailed as a Cadet under Captain North and he ended his cable with a simple prayer ... "May the sea bear them kindly".

An annual event in my life concerned the nearest Sunday to St. George's Day, the 23rd April, when on Merseyside we remembered the Zeebrugge Raid. It was a special day for the

Royal Marines. I was involved with the Royal Marine Reserves in their splendid headquarters at Morpeth Dock in Birkenhead.

The objective of the raid on Zeebrugge was to block the exits from the German submarine pens by sinking a cruiser, filled with concrete. It was almost a foolhardy enterprise, as the mole was scaled by ladders placed against it from the decks of the Birkenhead Ferries, the Iris and the Daffodil. It was slaughter. The Royal Marines never forgot the experience ... the 23rd April 1918.

The Service was held aboard the Royal Iris and was attended by folk from all over the country. There was always a Marine Band to fill the ferry with nautical tunes as we sailed down the Mersey. Never was "Eternal Father" better sung! Wreaths were laid on the waters and, even though the raid had taken place back in 1918, well into the 1970's we had marines who had actually been at Zeebrugge. The Marine Corps has a strong sense of Brotherhood and I expect the annual Zeebrugge Parade will continue into the next century. The day always ended with a march-past at Wallasey Town Hall, followed by a ham tea with apple tart and icecream. It must have been a great occasion because most of the ladies wore hats in the early years!

Two characters have etched themselves into my life ... Gordon Hector Tholen and Frank Hope Holland, both Master Mariners. When Gordon was at school, he was told to forget scholastic activity, but years later he met the teacher who had made that judgement.

"And what are you doing now, Tholen?"

"Teaching spherical trigonometry at a College".

Because of my dog collar, Gordon did not tell me what the old teacher said in reply. He was a natural communicator at the Byrom Street Nautical College with lectures punctuated with jokes and the board covered with funny drawings. Off to sea at sixteen, he paid his own way at college, bought his own books and paid for all his exams. It's the way it was! Like all the other men who took their tickets, he sat for his Medical Exams with Doctor Murray

Cearns and was told, "When in doubt turn to the last page of the medical book ... Burial at Sea!" After teaching in Byrom Street, for twenty years he was the Chief of the National Dock Labour Training School in Liverpool. The dockers called him Acker Bilk - "Stranger on the shore". His dog sat behind his desk when Gordon was elsewhere. The dockers said. "That dog needs a psychiatrist - he don't know whether he's a docker or a staff member!" Much instruction in the country was based on his text book ideas. He even started dockers with evening classes in art and other subjects! Above all, he kept me topped up with stories. God bless him!

Frank Hope Holland was naturally called Dutchy. At sea at sixteen in 1931, he was to cross the Atlantic many times during the war. In 1942, he came ashore to take his master's ticket at Byrom Street and must have impressed them, because he was taken on as a temporary lecturer and stayed for twenty-nine years. He was a great man. When his pal, Gordon, died, Frank clutched my hand.

"A prayer, padre!"

I had been called Bob for many years, but then he needed me as a padre. I prayed for our old friend. Then Frank relaxed.

"That's alright now."

That said it all about the man. God will use him well. Frank loved animals and wrote a Prayer for Animals.

> Dear Lord, look on us here below
> And give us friends who kindness show,
> Tis not for much that we do ask,
> To care for us is small a task.
> Each day fresh drink and food to eat
> A shelter from the cold and heat
> A little exercise and fun
> It's such a joy to have a run;

A daily groom to keep me clean
And that is all so it would seem.
But most of all we need a friend
To care for us until the end.

That was dedicated to Jason, Amber, Elsa, Honey, Carla, Amber II, Brit and Tao (the cat).

Almost five years after retirement and just a week before we returned to live in Liverpool, the Daily Post on Tuesday June 7th carried a front page headline by Janice Rowe, which spun my memories back some fourteen years.

"FOUND: SHIP IN TRAGIC RIDDLE"

The article went on to describe how a broken vessel had been located 2.8 miles under the ocean. Was it the Derbyshire?

One of the saddest stories of my career was the loss of the Derbyshire. She was part of the Bibby Group and, in July 1980, loaded a cargo of iron ore concentrates in the port of Seven Islands, Quebec Province, Canada, for discharge in Japan. She sailed on July 12th and on August 6th was at Capetown taking on stores and mail.

A month later, on September 6th, the Master, Captain Geoffrey Underhill, sent a radio message to the Company giving the ship's estimated time of arrival at Kawasaki, Japan as September 11th. Two days later, he radioed that the arrival would be delayed as bad weather had been encountered. Finally on September 9th, in what was to be the last recorded communication, he reported the Derbyshire was "hove to", that is, making no headway in a severe tropical storm in a position some 700 nautical miles South-South West of Tokyo Bay.

A radio message to the ship from the Company's agent in Japan was acknowledged as having been received on board on September

9th. That message asked the Master for his estimated time of arrival in port. By Saturday, the 13th, no reply having been received, the agents were becoming increasingly concerned. Inquiries were made of various Far Eastern radio stations and, when it became clear that there had been no radio contact with the ship later than September 9th, the Japanese Maritime Safety Agency was alerted and asked to commence an immediate air search of the area of the Derbyshire's last reported position. Ships arriving in and sailing from Japan were also asked to keep a close look-out for her. The air search continued until September 20th when, after further storms in the area, it was abandoned.

On September 22nd, the Company was obliged to acknowledge with great sadness that the vessel was lost, presumably foundered in the storm with the loss of all the ship's company, the forty-four souls aboard.

Again we were asked to hold an immediate informal Service at Pier Head and the sadness was deep as each man had come from Merseyside. Many hundreds attended and all the seafarers' Chaplains took part in the simple Act of Remembrance.

Some weeks later a Service took place in the Anglican Cathedral and my task was to read the names. Anguish, hope, prayer and despair seemed to punctuate the silences between each of the names, as the families remembered their loved ones.

Well over a decade later, the families still continue to meet in the Mission and I cannot speak too warmly of the British Sailors' Society Chaplain, Peter McGrath, as he meets with them and shares their love. I think that it is significant that they now call themselves the "Derbyshire Family" and we might all learn from the way in which they support each other. They really are a family.

In the years which have followed, there has been much speculation, and rightly so, as the next of kin ask their questions. The recent discovery of the wreck might at last reveal the truth.

Lloyds Intelligence Service actually recorded from 1980 to 1985 the loss of sixteen large ships with over four hundred lives in equally mysterious circumstances. No evidence has been found to account for these tragedies.

Millions of us sat in front of the television on the 15th April 1989 to watch Liverpool play a F.A. Cup match at Hillsborough in Sheffield. As the game started, the cameras moved to the crowd, which at one end was in turmoil. As the fans climbed over the fences, others were being crushed against the barriers. The nation watched as 95 were killed.

My memory of the Memorial Service in Liverpool Cathedral is of one solitary choirboy processing the full length of the nave, singing unaccompanied, "You'll never walk alone", which was the Liverpool theme song on the Kop. I doubt whether there was a dry eye in the whole congregation, but the sentiment was correct. We are never alone.

We sailed one afternoon from Morpeth Dock aboard the Royal Navy's Auxiliary vessel, "Loyal Watcher". Her draught was slight and, as we set out for the Bar, I knew that we would bob and weave our way down channel. With us were two young ladies from the Girls' Nautical Corps, complete with bugles. Also aboard were a dozen veterans from the Coastal Services Association and we were intent on holding a Memorial Service for comrades long departed. The ship was built strictly for work in the estuary, her task to search for mines in wartime.

When two of the veterans were dismally ill in a bucket, we all decided with no vote to abandon our intrepid voyage to the Bar Light and get on with it. That was the most sensible thought during the entire outing. The weather was very unkind!

I wrapped my arm around a convenient stay, whilst the ship's company was called to order. As soon as I started the Service, the faces of our two female buglers went paler and, if possible, a little more green. The ship was doing unforgivable things, so I hurried on to the Last Post, which was played with accuracy and increasing tempo. The girls made it and promptly disappeared. The blessing, a flat-bottomed turn of the ship and we set out to return to dry land.

With our stern to the weather, the movement was transformed and I found myself leaning over the side discussing Haydn Symphonies at some length ... there are over one hundred of them! Then we moved on to the submarine service in the last war.

I shall ever be grateful for that conversation with Arthur McArdle. I told him that my elder brother had been lost in the submarine Thistle in the early months of the war and all the information that we received was that he was "missing presumed dead". Arthur explained how to obtain more details from our sources and from the German archives. Three weeks later we had the story.

Thistle had sailed from Scapa on the 7th April 1940 for the Skagerrak off Norway. Two days later, they sighted the German submarine U4. Six torpedoes were fired, but U4 dived and all six missed. Two days on, the tables were turned, when U4 caught Thistle on the surface, charging her batteries. The German U-boat fired two torpedoes and Thistle was sunk. Five officers and forty-eight men died. One of them was Chief Petty Officer Frank Evans, my elder brother.

In the information that I received, it was recorded that on the 10th April 1940 at 0212, U4, commanded by Hans Peter Hinsch had torpedoed Thistle. Then details were presented of the career of this Captain, but they did not state whether he survived the war.

In 1965, I was chatting in the lounge of the Mission to a man, whom I chanced to discover had been a submariner. His name was Arthur Briard and in 1940 he had been the youngest crew member in Thistle! He had missed that last fatal voyage because of a severe cold. We became friends and he spent some time with my young family, although after a few years he disappeared from Merseyside. We never saw or heard from him again.

Although the loss of the Thistle was a long time ago, I can never forget that my sister-in-law, Zena, received the princely widow's pension of twenty-five shillings a week for herself and her two daughters, Kay and Diane, who were both under three. It seemed to make a mockery of "We will remember them".

One of the greatest opportunities that can be afforded a parson is the privilege of being asked to conduct a funeral for a loved one. In this way I met some remarkable families. It is sad that so many of the stories are not written and that the legacy of the past is so quickly forgotten. One such story should have started in Greenwich.

Over many years I had involved myself with the Sea Cadet Units on Merseyside and was Chaplain to the Central Unit. As a result of all this, I was asked to attend a conference at the Royal Naval College at Greenwich.

Only those who have worshipped in the College Chapel can understand the real beauty and majesty of the building, especially in the early morning hours. However, the high spot of that week was the "Dining-in-Night" in the Painted Hall. After an excellent meal, the port was circling, the "loyal toast" behind us, when the Mess President was joined by the Band Master. We raised our glasses to the musicians and thumped our tables, until the Band Master stood on top of the High Table and at a merry tempo played the Post Horn Gallop. Tradition is impressive when you are in the middle of it.

We were invited to spend an afternoon in the National Maritime Museum, which is vast and wonderful. I selected to inspect, for the allocated two and a half hours, the horological department as my guided tour. The time passed quickly! With hindsight, I should have chosen the Medal Room.

In that Room I might have seen a Croix de Guerre with Bronze Palm, which had been awarded to a small Naval vessel in 1944. That would have been the link between Greenwich, France, Liverpool and my story.

The small Naval vessel was H.M.S. Tarana, an armed trawler, which played a vital part in the drama of espionage, evasion and escape in the South of France. Her Captain was Edward Burling Clark, Lieutenant- Commander, R.N.R. When his daughter, Rosemary Fitzpatrick, asked me to conduct his funeral some forty years later, I was able to uncover the remarkable story.

Captain Edward Burling Clark

During the year 1942, H.M.S. Tarana would sail from Gibraltar, black hull, grey upper works and funnel, White Ensign flying ... just another armed trawler going about her business. But, once the Rock had dipped over the horizon, all hands were mustered. She was repainted to look like a fishing trawler, gear was strewn about the deck and all the men dressed like fishermen. Over the stern hung a tattered French, Moroccan or Spanish flag. This was Tarana's war rig!

The Pat O'Leary Organisation, together with a Polish group, ran a very successful escape line and Tarana was part of the system. Many hundreds of men and women were brought safely out of France. On the return journey to Gibraltar, the disguise was reversed and Tarana became a Naval ship.

One person brought out in this way was Airey Neave, who when he was Ulster spokesman for the Tories, declared that the Provisional Sinn Fein should be banned. Just two years later, when he was a Senior Aide to Mrs Thatcher, as he arrived at the underground car park at the House of Commons, a terrorist bomb killed him. He had continued to advocate a tough line on the I.R.A. and his death was to mark the start of another major campaign of terrorism.

This was the calibre of man and woman that Captain Clark was rescuing from France. I knew Captain Clark well, but had no idea of his story. Whilst his activities received no award from his own country, he was awarded the Croix de Guerre with Gold Star by France and the Polish Cross of Swords.

He was born in Birkenhead in 1902. His first job was in the accounts department of the Mersey Docks and Harbour Board, but he soon went to sea with Elder Dempster. At the age of twenty-five, he was an Extra-Master, sailing with White Star and, then, with the Belfast Steamship Company. In 1928, he spent a year with the Fleet as a R.N.R. Officer in the Mediterranean. In 1939, he joined the Fleet in Scapa Flow and, in no time, was involved with Atlantic patrols. Then followed the Gibraltar exploits. By the end of the war, he was serving in India.

On returning to England, he resumed his work with the Belfast Steamship Company and became the Master of the Ulster Prince and the Ulster Monarch, proudly flying his Blue Ensign. By that time he was the Commodore of the Line. He finally retired in 1967.

At the time of his death in 1981, I had known Nobby Clark for twenty years. He never talked of his adventures, but I am pleased to be able to tell a little of his story.

There were so many others like Captain Clark, whose stories will never be told.

So many to remember ... we forget at our peril.

18. 🏃

Good Sport

There must be a Taiwanese word or two for "putting the shot", but unfortunately I never came across it. And I never did master how to explain to a Chinese crew that I required them to run a relay race with four men, each one running one hundred metres and to do it one after the other. I knew that I had failed when all four arrived at the tape together!

Yet, we always succeeded in organising a Sport's Week. Many a seafarer sailed away from Liverpool with a puzzled frown, taking with him what, in ecclesiastical terms, is described as "a cloud of unknowing". All this odd activity would take place in such places as the Jeffrey Humble Sports Ground on Long Lane and might be better described as "we have ways of making you enjoy yourselves".

It always rained. They all complained that I could probably walk on the stuff, but they had problems. I put my success down to one item ... wellies!

In fairness to the Taiwanese, whilst they could see the circle in which they were to stand, the landing area was at least three inches deep with water and the shot, as it landed, disappeared from sight. This was my big moment. With all my dog collar authority, I would step into the puddle and declare the exact point of landing. No-one argued. They all had one thought in mind. "It must be time to go back to the ship." I concluded that basically seafarers are not happy with water.

Every Sport's Week was a perfect example of ecumenism, which is the "posh" word for "working together". The British Sailors' Society, the Norwegian and Swedish Churches and ourselves, all pulled together under the expert guidance of Kjell Tviberg, who was a Sport's Officer with the Norwegian Government Seamen's Service. Kjell was a tremendous character, who kept us on our toes. He expected us to be efficient. In fact, without Kjell and the two delightful secretaries, who came with him from Norway, the Sport's Week could never have been held. It took many meetings and weeks of preparation before the opening day and we always ended the week with a party and prize-giving in the Mission.

My fondest memory was standing at the Long Jump pit with the crew list of every man off the Yugoslavian ship, Plitvice, and naturally it was raining. Alongside were all our helpers with measuring tape and sand rakes.

It was my privilege to call out the names of the competitors. This was no mean task, as each name was at least ten letters long and they all ended with "inski". That was not quite correct, because one of the fourteen of the crew on the Plitvice was called Mr King. You could not miss him. He chanced to be from Nigeria. No-one ever explained how he happened to be on board.

In a clear voice, I called out, "Mr King". He leaped to his feet, flung his arms out wide and announced to the whole world, "I am the King". All the crew of Plitvice jumped to their feet, turned as a man towards him and bowed. This apparently was a ritual on his ship and, thereafter, whenever his name was called, everyone on the sport's field made obeisance. All North Liverpool must have thought we were entertaining Royalty.

I discovered that he was the cook in the ship and I quietly hoped that he was a better cook than he was a long jumper. Nothing was more embarrassing than watching that cook ambling up the runway as my helpers chanted, "Here comes the King!" Happily this was met with full approval and in every event he entered, he was greeted in this way. At least the rain had stopped for a while.

Football was an essential ingredient of every afternoon and all the ships were involved. This was quite an effort. There was one week when we involved 572 competitors, off 20 ships, embracing 15 nations.

The Nigerians, off the "River Rima", were playing the Koreans off the "Eastern Unicorn", which was on charter to Canpac, travelling between Liverpool and Montreal. Incidentally, the "River Rima" was still under arrest, so the crew was delighted to have a break off the ship.

The Captain of the "Eastern Unicorn" was standing alongside me, as we watched the match. He looked at his watch, turned to me and said, "Take me back to the ship, padre, so we can collect the food for the crew". I was somewhat surprised, but was ever obliging and together we set out for the West wall of the Royal Seaforth Dock.

The ship was almost new and was a lovely sight, as she towered above the quayside. The height of the gangway was a challenge and I made a mental note that there was no way in which I would volunteer to carry the food. We arrived at the Master's cabin, via the galley, and much climbing of stairways. He asked me to remove my shoes and to leave them in the companionway. The reason became obvious. His carpet was thick-piled and luxurious and spotlessly white. As we waited for the food, I was shown remarkable photographs of the wonders of Korea and told about the excellence of the Hyundai car. He was proud of his country and rightly so. His ship was immaculate and every man aboard was dressed in a smartly-cut blue battle-dress. It was good to share all this with him.

At last the food was ready, and as we returned down the gangway, I saw the canisters had already been placed alongside the Mission van. So we headed back to the football match.

The game was still being fought and I naturally assumed that we would wait for the final whistle. I was wrong. The Captain stood about five feet two inches, a small man, but he strode purposefully on to the pitch, held up his arms and shouted in Korean, "Stop the match!" At least, I suspect that was what he had said. It worked well. As a man, the Koreans stopped in their tracks and picked up the ball. The referee blew his whistle. He also waved his arms and in strangled Scouse said, "But, gentlemen, you cannot do that!" That, of course, was my interpretation.

We carried the canisters on to the pitch. Not only both teams, but everyone present on the ground, shared the lovely food which had been provided. That explained the delay on the ship, as the Captain had made sure that there was enough for all. My staff, in the mysterious way that I was not supposed to understand, produced innumerable cans of ale. The match was declared a draw and we enjoyed ourselves. Not for the first time I was experiencing the brotherhood of the sea, which cuts across all nationalities, colours and creeds. I believe that everyone present felt exactly that.

Each year the International Sports Committee for Seafarers produced a glossy brochure with all the results tabulated from all the major ports in the world. This was the report on Liverpool in that year.

"Sports Cements Friendship"

"The weather was not kind to the organisers of the International Sport's Week in Liverpool. Nevertheless, well over 300 seafarers left their ships to take part in athletics and football.

"Such a Sport's Week proves of value, not just as a physical event, but cements friendship and co-operation. The prize-giving ceremony to end the week was a great event with 120 seafarers present. But before the festivities, seafarers from 21 ships of 13 nationalities competed for the medals and honours.

"Two Russian ships, Paide and Vaigach, were placed first in the team championship, Class 1, with Baider Fortuna, Japan, in third place. Craigavad, FRG, and Plitvice, Yugoslavia, climbed to the top of the final standings in Class 2. The Yugoslavians from Plitvice were only beaten by a local Engineering School, North East Tech, in the 4 by 100 metres relay. Paide, USSR, kept a British trio from the M/V Rubens, 3/10ths of a second behind in the 3 by 60 metres relay."

Prize-giving

The final prize-giving night in the Mission was one to remember. Carlsberg were generous with free lager and that avoided the embarrassment for the Russians, whose roubles could not be negotiated by the bank. Our Chairman, David Lowry, was on excellent form and with the assistance of Trevor Furlong, the Managing Director of the Mersey Docks and Harbour Company, the evening went with a swing. The food was excellent and the Week was voted a winner.

It was a rare privilege to have the ships' companies off two Russian vessels. They sat together and occupied a corner of the lounge. Prominent among them was the Commissar. You could not miss him, as he sat alone.

Visiting the Russian ships had always been good for a laugh in my early days. Then I would be stopped at the head of the gangway by a large, fierce-looking character. I believe these men were specifically produced for the job.

"What do you want?"

"I've come to visit the ship's company."

"Niet!"

"May I see the Commissar?"

That never failed and I would be led along companionways up to the cabin.

The Commissar was the "Big Brother" on board and his task was to control the political discipline. That was the only form of discipline, as far as I could see. The Master of the ship was really the Senior Navigating Officer. I assumed that was why we occasionally found female senior officers, but I never, at that time, was given the opportunity to inquire closely.

So I appeared before the Commissar to be examined.

"What do you want?"

There was a good response to that and I invariably used it.

"I've called to see the Christians aboard."

The result was always the same as the party line was produced. It was like putting a penny into a slot machine.

There are no Christians in this ship!"

That was when I trotted out my party line.

"That's odd. There must be many thousands of Christians in Russia. I would expect one or two ... "

I rarely was allowed to finish such a sentence. The Commissar would be on his feet.

"You must go now."

And go I did, with the smell of the salt mines in the air.

All that changed in the middle sixties. Thereafter, we were able to visit quite freely, although at that time they would not come near the Mission. Our Christianity was too obviously on display for them, but it did not prevent them from enjoying coach trips and football.

There was one morning when a Russian Captain and his Chief Engineer came into my study. Over coffee, they explained that they had passed their sister ship in mid-Atlantic and the out-going Master had told them of our activities. I explained the pleasure it would give us to help them, called in "Mr Russell" and organised yet another cultural tour. Apart from local sight-seeing, we sometimes reached York, the Lakes or Llandudno. This time it was to be Chester.

If there was time, we made sure that they, not only walked the Walls of Chester, but also visited the Cathedral. We wondered what they would talk about when they returned home and liked to think that we were doing our little bit to foster world peace, not that they were ever belligerent. They might even have been sorry for us as we struggled "under the heel of capitalism".

That prize-giving evening was much enjoyed by the Russians off the Paide and Vaigach. The lounge was full. When the winning competitors came forward to receive the cups and medals, laughter held the evening together, as we pulled each other's legs and imitated each other's language. Through it all, the Commissar sat stone-faced and silent. He pretended that he spoke no English, which was a nonsense. Even the Russians ignored him.

The date was August 23rd 1987 and we knew that the wind of change was sweeping across Eastern Europe. No-one could have guessed at that time that the ultimate change would be so swift and far-reaching. Yet the signs were there that evening. When the presentations were over, to our delight, the Russians presented each person there with a lapel badge, which was inscribed with the name of their home port, Tallin. We wore them with pride.

There had been very many Sport's Weeks and it was pleasing to visit ships and chat about the cups and trophies on display in the Messes. Sport can bring us together.

Russell Thomas, a seafarer & self in earnest discusion

19.

At Peace

I have forgotten the number of times that I have been asked by a hospital patient the blunt question, "Am I going to die?" I never hesitated with my reply, "Yes, of course you are, like the rest of us!" Then we could talk.

In my pocket, I always carried a printed card and it proved its worth many times. On it were the thoughts of Henry Scott Holland (1847-1918), who had been a Canon of St. Paul's Cathedral.

"Death is nothing at all. I have only slipped away into the next room. I am I, and you are you. Whatever we were to each other, that we still are. Call me by my old familiar name, speak to me in the easy way which you have always used. Put no difference in your tone, wear no forced air of solemnity or sorrow. Laugh as we always laughed at the little jokes we enjoyed together. Pray, smile, think of me, pray for me. Let my name be ever the household word that it ever was. Let it be spoken without effect, without the trace of a shadow on it. Life means all that it ever meant. It is the same as it ever was; there is unbroken continuity. Why should I be out of mind because I am out of sight? I am waiting for you, for an interval, somewhere very near, just around the corner. All is well."

That was always helpful. The fear is rarely death itself. The real concern was for the rest of the family and the well-being of the loved ones.

I thought it sad, when the patient knew that his days were numbered as did the family, but the game of pretence was maintained by everyone. Lies were told and the real cares and worries of the patient were lost in the half-world of deceit

"Please, don't tell them."

Whilst wishes have to be respected, the parson is well placed to challenge them.

The easiest and happiest of partings have been when the truth is shared and the future discussed. Of course, no parting is simple. The emergence of the Hospice to care for the dying with dignity and love does bring peace and understanding to all involved, including the medical and nursing staff.

For the seafarer there was never the chance of normality, no warning for the family and little more than silence from all around.

You never forget the first time that you are asked to break news of death at sea. The telephone call was from the Company agent in London and gave just the basic facts. A young seaman in Rosario in South America had missed the cutter, which was to return him and other shipmates to the ship out in the river. They decided to "borrow" a dinghy! Little did they realise the strength of the tide and the currents. The dinghy capsized and they were all lost. That was the message that I had been asked to convey to the next of kin.

I had enough common-sense to call next door to check on the condition of the man's wife. It was a wise precaution. She was eight months pregnant. I discovered where the mother lived in Liverpool, collected her, and together we broke the terrible news. That task was never to grow easier.

Quickly I learned that you must never go alone, when the situation is unknown. My impression after this long passage of time is not of trauma, but of the immense courage of people in the face of tragedy. Too often once the news was given, some families seemed to enter a state of unbelief, because the death was so far away. In many instances there was be no body, and there never would be.

This meant that there was no funeral. It was as though the voyage had been extended and was going on for ever ... in any case he was not expected back for a month or so! By that time, most friends would no longer be supportive. People forget too quickly.

There was no way in which I could give long term support; so I had to ensure that the local caring community would take over. It was always necessary to alert the particular brand of clergyman preferred and also make sure that the extended family was alerted. The bearer of the sad news can be an embarrassment.

My next opportunity to help would come a few weeks later, when I would return to assist with the application forms for the various charities and trusts which were concerned with the orphaned and the bereaved.

Details for wreaths were sent through the shipping company or agent, when the cremation or burial was overseas. It was also necessary to contact the chaplain who would conduct the Service, so that photographs might be taken and sent to the next of kin. I often accompanied a local shipping agent as all the details were sorted.

There was one strange occasion when I heard of an accident aboard a ship from the television and within minutes the telephone rang to tell me about the explosion and the details of the death for the next of kin. The ship's name had been given and the families of every crew member would have been fearing the worst. I telephoned a vicar, who lived almost next door to the bereaved, and within ten minutes I called the agent. He contacted the B.B.C. in time for the announcer to state that the next of kin had been informed. It must have brought relief to the other families.

Christmas was always a more difficult time. There was one Christmas Day when, on three occasions, I went out with news of a tragedy in different parts of the world. Perhaps the trauma is better understood, when you realise that most seafarers are aged from sixteen to thirty.

I was ever grateful for the support afforded by the Royal Liverpool Seamen's Orphan Institution, which specialised in relief to the fatherless and orphaned children of British seamen, by providing for their maintenance and clothing and "furthering their education by grants according to individual needs and circumstances". This last care continued from the cradle to adulthood and was of immense value. A telephone call to Les Dodd was all that was required. I believe that all of us enjoyed their annual get-together, which started with a formal A.G.M. in Liverpool Town Hall and ended in the Nautical Catering College with good food and much chat and laughter.

Another great support came from Bill Kirkwood of the Sailors' Children's Society at the Newlands Homes in Hull. Again, the financial help covered every orphan and even provided homes for the homeless.

It was to Valerie Austin of the Shipwrecked Mariners' Society that we turned to for advice and financial assistance for those in trouble. As we acted as the local agent, we were able to give speedy help when needed.

The bereaved are quickly forgotten. Death is treated as though it were an illness.

"Why doesn't she pull herself together!"

I felt that it was necessary to visit the home, when others had stopped. Whilst I was there to talk about practical matters, we could naturally talk about the man with an understanding of the way of life and with a knowledge of the difficulties facing as seafarer's widow.

Pain cannot be swept aside. It must be met with love and that we can share. I never said that I understood. It is not possible to understand. To say so is almost making light of the pain. You can show love.

Many feel uncomfortable and will not mention the name of the deceased in case they "upset" the widow. It is strange to pretend that a person never existed, especially as he is the only person the bereaved wishes to remember.

Often I was asked to take the funeral or the Memorial Service, because over the years I had become the family chaplain. It was a friendship which crossed all colours and creeds. Sometimes it was not possible to meet the particular brand of spirituality, and I was called in to fill the gap.

Committing ashes to the sea

There was much to learn. In the West, we have little concept of weeping and wailing. One afternoon, I found myself in a house, just off Upper Parliament Street, breaking the news of death at sea of a Nigerian cook. He lived in Percy Street. The neighbours came into the house in numbers and the wailing began. It meant that the family could sob unashamedly and you could almost feel the release of tension and emotion. I was defeated by it all, having been well schooled in the stiff upper lip in the face of death. I suspect that our approach leads to deep emptiness and, in the months ahead, the eventual breakdown, when all had stopped caring. The more emotion that you hold in, the more people think that "you have got over it" and the less support is given. You are alone.

It felt strange to be the only Christian, leading an Act of Remembrance, surrounded by the spiritual overtones of the Hindu or the Moslem. I confess that I was to find a deeper spiritual awareness than was exuded from many a Parish Church, not that I totally understood what was happening.

Sometimes pieces of hair and finger nails were cut, carefully packed, and sent by post to the next of kin overseas. If possible, I would enclose a letter with as many details as I could find, describing the Act of Remembrance or the funeral, and also writing a prayer for them to use. I assumed that the letter would be read aloud.

During the ceremonies, I would draw aside, or if possible into another room, so that the mourners could come forward to express their thoughts in different languages and customs. Rites were performed with salt and water and strange incantations. I never understood why one group, with no prior warning, came forward in the crematorium, whilst I was in full flow, and solemnly placed a pair of shoes on the coffin. Maybe my antics were seen as equally odd and I, too, would be given the benefit of the doubt. We certainly are all different.

Once I was standing at the graveside, surrounded by Chinese and I had just reached the words, "Earth to earth, ashes to ashes, dust to dust", when with a resounding crump the sides of the grave collapsed in on the coffin. The ground shook. All the Chinese took a pace back in awe and I suspect that my standing went up a notch or two in the vicinity of Great George's Square and China Town.

One widow, who was a good Anglican, asked that I take Quaker devotions at the crematorium, as her husband had been leaning in that direction. My inquiries about rites were not very fruitful, but I did glean that silence was the main ingredient. That, on the face of it, was not very helpful. So, we recited the Twenty-Third Psalm with, by my watch, one minute of silence between each verse. You have no idea how long a minute is until you try this exercise. The tension in the Chapel was immense and, as we departed, everyone expressed their appreciation of such a meaningful service. Maybe we should all stop and think about that particular experience.

Normally the only time an Anglican parson is silent is when he cannot find the right place in the book and then hears himself saying to the congregation, "Let us keep a moment of silence". Even worse, when the parson intends a silence to be kept, he spends five minutes telling the poor congregation what they should be pondering. The verbal garbage and ecclesiastical platitudes in which we indulge are alien to real life ... I am as guilty as anyone. We certainly talk too much. Is silence really golden?

Happily, humour is very close to sadness. An early morning telephone call resulted in the doubtful joy of climbing the filthy and over-smelly stairs of a tower block in Netherton.

At last I found the right floor and the right door. The lady led me into the kitchen and we sat at the table, surrounded by the debris of the week's instant food and a bottle of whisky. It was ten in the morning. I told my tale as best I could and I think she grasped the tragedy.

"Have a drink, love".

Refusal was too late. The tumbler was half full. A gentleman, not introduced, had sat in silence on the other side of the table. The widow seemed little moved by my story, chatted about the broken lift and the state of the stairs, and kept the glasses full. I ignored the whisky and was a bit mesmerised. I assumed it was due to her emotional state.

"He was not my husband, you know!"

I had not been trained for such a moment, so remained silent.

"I've had two real husbands and four sort of."

At ten in the morning, as she pulled her dressing gown yet again together, there had been occasional, unfortunate glimpses of her charms. I had begun to realise that husband number seven was being fully primed with whisky opposite me and that he only had one dilemma. Was he going to be a "real" or a "sort of"? It was as well that I had not touched the whisky.

At last I attempted to make my escape to the Mission van and its student driver, but she had not quite finished with me. She put her hand on my sleeve and uttered the words, which have become one of our family sayings.

"I trust God likes a good trier!"

At the end of it all, each one of us might accept that as our epitaph.

20. GEENA

Mainly Birds

The daily routine meant arriving before nine each morning, so that we might say Matins together in the Chapel. That was not always possible, but remained as one of my paving stones on the heavenly journey. I enjoyed it in Kingston House when we had two or three students and two Assistant Chaplains. After Matins, we would spend half an hour discussing the next chapter of the book which we were all studying together. One of us would present the appropriate chapter and lead the discussion. It was amazing the number of solid tomes we managed to absorb in this way. In the middle of such a discussion one morning, the Chapel door opened and a porter made an announcement.

"One of you lot had better come to the reception."

It was a Greek seafarer, slightly agitated.

Languages, on paper, are comparatively easy to tackle, until you try them out on the natives. They always talk too quickly and use long words. I survived in Greek with my Classical and Hellenistic clerical background. At least on this occasion it worked well enough for me to get the name of the man's ship. The Journal of Commerce told me that the ship was a tanker at Dingle Jetty. As our conversation was not improving, I decided that I would take him back to his vessel, where I would find someone to help with the language barrier and hopefully sort out his problem. So I bundled him into the Mission van and set forth for Dingle Oil

Jetty, some two miles south of Pier Head.

In the van, I decided to try my best Welsh German and was delighted when he responded in some sort of Greek German. In quick time, I discovered that his ship was sailing at ten that morning. I drove faster and he spoke faster.

Arriving at the Dingle, I was a little upset to find that his ship was sitting in the middle of the river. He was waving his arms and looking up to heaven. I dashed into one of the offices in order to telephone the Port Radar Station. They came back with the message from the ship.

"The ship's cutter is coming to the landing stage at Pier Head at ten to collect the crew."

Obviously our attempt at communicating in a mutual language was not very accurate.

I stuffed my seafarer back into the van and we took off at a rate of knots. By this time he was in full flow in what I assumed was an obscure Greek dialect, which necessitated violent arm actions. I gave up and concentrated on driving. I believe that I hold the unofficial speed record between Dingle Jetty and the Liverpool Landing Stage, although I share it with a Greek seafarer. We motored down the floating roadway as the Liver clock struck ten.

At the far end of the Stage was a small bunch of seafarers. My passenger had me firmly by the arm as he marched me towards them. Words were exchanged and the Mate in immaculate English turned upon me.

"Why have you been driving this man around Liverpool at a furious rate for the last half an hour?"

I did my best to explain, realising that the Greek had not grasped my intention as we had set out on my breath-taking drive to the Dingle and back. I reached the word, "problem", in my explanation and was stopped sharply.

"This is a nonsense! He merely came into the Mission to ask a question. He was at the dance last night and lost his cuff link.

He wondered if you found it."

I must confess that I backed away as quickly as possible, but was told that for the rest of the day I walked around muttering that I should have found the Greek word for "cuff link".

Ignorance of a language is a poor excuse, but I ever tried. My greeting in Spanish invariably elicited the prompt response. "Why don't we speak English?" In fact English is the language of the sea and the air and these days the Russians and Chinese all wish to practice their English. This almost totally removed the motivation to communicate in anything else but the mother tongue. Even a German once asked me, "And where did you learn to speak English, boyo?" It is not always easy to be Welsh.

A ward Sister in Clatterbridge, which is over the water in Wirral about twenty miles away, called me on the telephone.

"We've a Spanish seafarer in our ward who speaks no English."

"Do you want an interpreter to help the medical staff?"

"That's not the problem. Tomorrow is his eighteenth birthday. What can you do about it?"

"We'll be over at two o'clock".

A call to a Spanish ship was the first move. The patient's vessel had long sailed. The next day I arrived at the ship as arranged at one o'clock. Three men were lined up, dressed in their best suits and looking very smart. I did wonder what their black hair, white teeth and broad smiles would do for the junior nursing staff. Even though they had never met the sick man, they had visited George Henry Lee's in the morning and, on behalf of their ship's company, had bought a present, which was bedecked with ribbons. I also spotted bottles of wine, tucked out of sight under their jackets. No alarm bells rang, so we set out on our errand of mercy.

I shall not forget that man's face when we arrived in the ward. A hospital on your eighteenth birthday can be a lonely place and, if you cannot communicate, it must have been miserable. The warmth of greeting was loud and all-embracing. It was very un-English.

189

The understatement would be to call it an "instant party". It was more like a bomb! The hospital tom-toms beat the message and the doctors came out of the woodwork, like flies to the jam pot. Suddenly there was no language barrier.

That was many years ago and I am sure that our Spanish patient has long left the sea. Probably he is now well married with a brood of bambinos, peccadilloes or whatever the Spanish word is for "a quiverful". Of one thing I am certain. When his compatriots begin to knock this country of ours, his response will be, "When I was there, it was not like that!" This is on the assumption that he could actually remember what happened that long day ago.

Bishop Michael spreads the Good News

I would hope that there were times when we brought a little light relief into the lives of our Bishops. A ship visit was always good for the morale, but not of necessity for the stomach. There were occasions when the inner group of seafarers would sit around the Bishop in order to talk to him, whilst an outer group sat listening to provide the applause. When we returned the following day, we were never left in doubt of the pleasure and spiritual uplift, which the Bishop's presence had given. They never forgot.

We suspect that Michael Henshall, the Bishop of Warrington, will remember his visit to the Korean ship, the M/V Future Express, and our good friend Captain Quinto.

Everyone tries to put on a good show. The Episcopal visit was booked often months in advance. Our lives are controlled by diaries. This meant that we had no idea of the ship when the date was fixed. It was a game of Russian roulette. We did not fail to find a ship to accommodate the Bishop at twenty-four hours notice, although we once changed venues with two hours warning. Rarely did that matter, because we liked to eat the normal fare of the menu and we provided the wine to aid digestion.

Captain Quinto was about to open a bottle in his day-cabin, when in flew a pigeon! We all ducked in alarm, but not the Captain. As we recovered, the pigeon was sitting, happily perched on the Captain's head. He had continued to wrestle with the cork screw, as though the arrival was quite normal. Naturally, we had an immediate topic for conversation.

"That's a pigeon."

"Yes."

"Is it a tame one?"

"No."

"Has it got a name?"

"Yes."

The conversation was not going well.

"Tell us the story."

Captain Quinto seemed relieved that at last here was a question worthy of attention.

The name of the bird was Geena and it had come aboard the Future Express in Australia with a broken wing. The Captain had rescued it and given it refuge in his cabin. There in the corner was a box, a blanket and a dish of water and food.

"Is that where he sleeps?"

He stopped again, intent on pouring the wine.

"What happened when he could fly again?"

That primed the Captain and he was off again.

Apparently, Geena began to find her way around the ship, between decks, into cabins and especially into the galley. Naturally the bird was welcome anywhere aboard and brought much pleasure to the ship's company, which had signed on for a year. There was no end of the supply of bird food and there was no danger of competition. Even a bird brain could grasp the advantages of staying aboard.

The next port of call was in Malaysia and everyone thought that Geena, like any intelligent Australian pigeon, would go walk-about. In fact, Geena went ashore with the Captain and, wherever the Captain walked, so Geena followed from tree to tree. When the ship sailed, Geena signed on for the voyage. Whilst at sea, Geena came up on deck, sat on the mast and, when the fancy took her, she became airborne. Eventually they all arrived on Merseyside and Geena was introduced to a Bishop.

"Let's take a photograph of Geena on the Bishop's head."

Not a brilliant idea, but it might have found its way into the Diocesan newspaper. We discussed possible headlines, but it was of no avail. Geena refused to co-operate. We reckoned that she had turned Hindu in Malaysia.

It was a good lunch. Geena arrived after about five minutes in time for the first course. She may have lacked spirituality, but had no hang-up over gluttony.

My only real contact with our feathered friends was equally peculiar. A seafarer called at my office, carrying a home-made bird cage.

"Keep an eye on this perisher, padre. I'm just up just off to meet the wife in town."

"What is it?"

"A peach-faced love-bird."

"Great!"

He never came back.

It was very pretty, a picture of greens and crimson, about the size of a robust sparrow. We knew nothing about peach-faced love-birds; so I bought a book. The opening paragraph said it all, "Love-birds have a murderous disposition". The children promptly called him Crippen. He was well named. The family developed a love-hate relationship, which meant that he loved us and we hated him in a loving way. His party trick was to disappear up Stephen's jumper and reappear down his arm or up his neck. He just bit me!

The first evening, when D'rene and I came home, it was disaster. One of our three offspring had taken pity on him and opened the cage. That was a mistake. Airborne, Crippen was lethal. Cleverly, he made use of the delft-shelf around the room. He walked behind each expensive plate and eased them off the shelf. We could have qualified as slip fielders for Lancashire. That evening we ate our meal all wearing hats, as he had displayed great skills as a dive bomber. Then came the final challenge. It took over an hour to get him back in the cage.

After many years, he ended his days with Jen and Basil Williams. His manners had improved a little, although he could still shred a letter in seconds.

Never again did I afford sanctuary to a feathered friend, and naturally I know of no other variety.

21.

The Ella Stamper Story

Friday afternoon is always longer than any other afternoon, but there was one which seemed to last for two days. It was October 1983. I was sitting at my desk, trying hard to read and not doze, when the telephone shattered my incipient repose. It was Alan Green, one of our River Pilots.

"Where are you, Alan?"

That was a fair question as the atmospherics on the line suggested Bangkok.

"Aboard the Tadeusy Ocioszynski."

"Say again."

"It's Polish! We're docking in Langton."

"Is there anything I can do for you?"

That was a foolish question and the response was inevitable.

"There's a bit of a problem."

I should have known better, because when anyone indicates a problem, it immediately becomes yours. I was right.

"Can you meet us at the West Langton at about 1630?"

And I knew that the wheel of fate was in full twiddle.

Nothing to me is more exciting than watching a large Merchant vessel come alongside with the minimum of fuss and a bump as gentle as a kiss. The crew seem to appear at the last moment. Two or three of the shore gang almost casually walk the ropes to the bollards, expectant faces gaze down at the quay and then it is done. The gangway is lowered and secured. Suddenly all action goes up a gear, as dockers emerge from sheds and the seamen aboard lock their doors like landlubbers. The bridge empties, engines stop and the sounds in ship change to a more gentle throb. It all happens with no-one apparently giving any orders.

Almost the first man that I met aboard was the First Mate, whom I called Dinko. I believe that his real name is Dinkoslavirinskivich or something like that. Dinko is easier. I had known him since he was a cadet. I was never at ease when foreigners kissed me on both cheeks. Into a bear hug we went before I could work out the Polish for "Ger off!"

"Any chance of a game of football on Sunday?"

I made a mental note to ask the staff to organise it, because the answer to such a request was always affirmative.

Invariably we booked a game into the Everton Leisure Centre, which is tucked into Great Homer Street behind the once notorious Scotland Road. This is famous Liverpool territory. Apparently the challenge once upon a time was to drink half a pint in every pub on Scottie Road and only those in elbow training could achieve it. These days the famous road has been gutted and abandoned to the motor car, although there are still glimpses of the past.

I recall one football match on the hard-standing pitch at the Everton Leisure Centre, when we had a Russian team playing a Brazilian team. We thought it a good idea for the foreigners to kick each other about a bit! Alongside me stood the dark-faced, long coated, Russian Commissar grimly willing his side to win. I noticed his glances at the colourful graffiti, which graced the walls and the "atomic fall-out" of muck from Paddy's Market down the street. We breathed in the aroma of hamburgers, onions and curry sauce from the food wagons around the Centre. I thought that this good Scouse flavour might be the equal of any Middle Eastern souk. He was not impressed. At last he could contain himself no longer and spoke with precise English.

"I notice that the Capitalists in your country enforce the workers to live in these conditions."

I really did not know what he was talking about as all that I could see was a brand new Leisure Centre surrounded by almost new tower blocks standing like match-boxes with windows. I gazed about me. The graffiti was beautifully executed and even though the spelling was original, it did prove the desire to write. Maybe the ankle deep debris was proof of affluence and of a flourishing market, full of fruit and vegetables and food. The only obvious capitalist that came to mind was Lord Derby and I thought he was a charming character, who would not have been responsible for the garbage on the street. Our lot had dropped all that!

As I was working all this out in my mind, the Commissar was still awaiting an intelligent response. I have long discovered that all that is required to any question is instant agreement and that it makes for a more peaceful life.

"Yes."

This must have pleased him.

"Da."

I assumed that the implication was that his lot were better with rubbish than our lot.

Back on my Polish ship, Dinko had taken me up top to meet the Captain. A tot of something was thrust into my hand ... probably lethal, and to be ignored. And there was Alan Green, the pilot. He introduced me to my "problem". Her name was Ella Boyce Stamper and this is her story in her own words.

"I am a dental surgeon, single, and at the age of 61 I felt the call to work in Africa. I sold my practice and arranged for one flat to be kept for my return. I went out with the Sudan Interior Mission to East Africa.

" When our founder with two others went there in 1893, his aim was to get into the interior where Christ was unknown and, at that time, the whole area just north of the coast to the edge of the Sahara was marked Soudain, the home of the black man. But neither Sudan or Ethiopia liked the title and it was changed to East Africa and West Africa.

"I went out for a year to set up a clinic in Addis Ababa and to treat the missionaries (at that time we were about 300 in East Africa in Sudan, Ethiopia and Somalia), their children (then 168 in the Mission School at Addis) and the Ethiopian staff of the Mission.

"The man who had been appointed was delayed and I stayed on from the early October until late May 1972. During this time I visited three down country stations and was shocked to see the awful and unnecessary suffering of the rural people due to almost entire lack of any dental service. The result was that I came home to England, collected goods and equipment and returned to Ethiopia with the aim of helping the country people, but I very soon realised that the need was so immense that the only way I could multiply myself was to go into teaching.

Ella in Phalombe Hospital, S. Malawe

"Through various stages the pattern became established that I would go into a rural area and set up a dental clinic and four men would be brought in, some from great distances, nearly always men as so few African women had the necessary educational background. These were taught Basic Dentistry. I liked the minimum of three months, but was glad if I was given longer. Basic Dentistry was the teaching of how to give a good injection, do an adequate extraction, scale teeth and teach oral hygiene, also differential diagnosis, dosage of drugs, etc.

"There is no use training in Africa unless one can provide the necessary instruments, etc., as these countries are mostly bankrupt and have not got the foreign currency to make any purchases. The profession gave instruments, and friends, mostly ex-patients, and relations gave money to buy and freight these out to Africa.

"After training, I would go into the trainee's area, set him up. see that he was given a room with a good light, etc. A notice would be given out in the church that a "tooth doctor" was coming and that now was their chance. Patients would pour in and in this way I could get the new man established in his own area and I would work with him for up to two or three weeks. I would return later to see that all was well, up-grade him, encourage him, ensure that the supply route for drugs was working and deal with any problems.

"I was almost 61 when I arrived in Addis and was 74 on my birthday going up the Suez Canal on my way home to retire. I served thirteen years in Africa. I did projects for many other Missions ... the American Presbyterian, the American Baptists, the Menonites from Pennsylvania, the Daughters of Charity at Mekele, the Medical Mission Sisters in Malawi, and the Swedish Philadelphians. So you see that I am ecumenical!

"Our cargo boat left Mombasa in October 1983 and six weeks later the Captain was told that there was a strike at Avonmouth and the ship was heading for Liverpool. This left me with a problem. I knew that there would be no-one to meet me and I was much further from home. I told the pilot my troubles. How could I get myself and lots of baggage to Hove? I would need a bank and as we were arriving at four on the Friday, how could I obtain money? All he said was, "I'll telephone Padre Bob Evans. He'll sort you out!"

Ella stood about five feet nothing as I winkled out her story.

"Is there anyone down at Hove that I can call to say that you are back?"

"No need", she said. "Can you find me someone with a lorry?"

"Ella, you've been in Africa too long! Don't worry. We'll get you home tomorrow."

Actually she did not look in the least worried!

The next morning we stuffed all her belongings into the Mission van and, as Ella walked down the gangway, all the crew was lined up at the ship's side and with smiles on their faces they all clapped. That was the kind of person she was.

After we had sorted out the bank, I gave Ella a farewell squeeze which I rather enjoyed! She looked up at me with a twinkle in her eyes and said, "Bob, when I came to Liverpool, I knew that the Lord would provide". She was right. Everything had been provided.

After some reflection, I had a theory about this "providing activity". Maybe there was no way that God could have organised it without the Mersey Mission to Seamen. I do not see that as blasphemy, but a simple truth. God always needs people with the right training and the willingness to do His work. Then the Lord can provide! If I could use very small print, I would add that God needs you, as you need Him.

22.

The Arm of the Law

Our work in the port of Garston goes back to the start of the century and the Mission building there was sold just after the last war, although it is still in use as a company's office. During my years the port was always busy and at any time there were at least eight ships of some thousand tons. Many of them were either coasting or on regular "taxi runs", each with an average of ten men aboard. At night when I lay in bed in Aigburth, we were near enough to the river to tell the state of the tide by the beat of the engines, as ships moved in and out of Garston.

The docks were almost part of the town and it was normal for children to play on the slopes overlooking the ships. One evening, a gang of youths started to throw stones at a Polish ship. The ship was still being worked and the men were on deck. Unfortunately, one crew member was struck on the head by a stone. Naturally some of the crew ran off the ship and gave chase to the youngsters.

Apparently they caught up with them in town and in the struggle to hold them, one lad was badly bruised. The boy's parents promptly went to the police and the result was that two of the Polish seafarers were ordered to appear before the Magistrates the next day.

The shipping agent contacted me and we were fortunate to find a solicitor who spoke Polish. You must imagine the deep fear of authority, which was felt aboard the ship and there was little that I could say to allay those fears. The facts of the case were clear.

In court the men just stood and were very frightened. But all was well. The police recited the details very clearly and fairly. After consulting his colleagues, the senior Magistrate explained that we must not take the law into our own hands. Then I was pleased to hear him apologising for the behaviour of the youngsters. He nodded in my direction and asked if I would convey an apology to the Captain of the ship. The police were asked to review the local security and a probation officer was asked to visit the homes of the two lads who had been involved.

It must have been a long half hour for those men, but I was proud of our courts. When, however, all the messages had been conveyed, I was not certain that any person on that ship felt that justice had been seen to have been done.

It was not a simple matter to control the entry of people into the Mission, although we attempted to restrict it to the seafarer and those involved in the industry and to those who were "helping to forward the purpose of the Mission".

One evening in Colonsay House, we had some thirty men sitting quietly in the lounge watching a video film or just chatting. Into the Club came two men and two girls, although it did not appear that they were together. They sat well apart after ordering their drinks. Russell, who was Club manager, had been alerted by the barman, and quickly realised that all was not right. He quietly asked the two men to finish their drinks and to leave because they were not seafarers and had no legal right to be with us. They left with no difficulties. Next, Russell asked the girls to leave. Again, there was no problem. An hour later the police arrived.

As the two girls had left Colonsay House, so had two Greek seafarers, leaving the rest of their crew to return to their ship by our mini-bus. In fact, the mini-bus had passed the two Greeks as they were strolling back to the docks about half a mile away. Then apparently the seamen were faced by the two men and the two girls. Without any words, one of the men attacked one seaman thrusting a knife into his stomach. The four youngsters ran away. Fortunately for the injured seaman, a passing motorist stopped and with great courage rushed him to Walton Hospital into the Intensive Care Unit. The police arrived at the Mission and asked for details and descriptions.

All this appeared in the local press and resulted in another man coming forward to reveal that he too had been attacked in the same area that evening, but had not been hurt.

Happily the injured man - the two Greeks were uncle and nephew - was not too badly hurt and was flown home a few days later. The Captain was very much on our side, because we always collected men off ships and returned them at the end of the evening. Yet again the Master stressed the folly of walking the dock roads at night, even though they are well lit and appear to be completely safe.

Eventually we heard that the assailants had been identified and caught. The C.I.D. Officer told me that the attacker was only aged fifteen, but looked much older. He came from a good home and the parents were amazed to learn of their stupidities. When asked why they had made the assault, the youngster said, "It was my turn to use the blade!"

I have no idea how you can deal with such a mental attitude. It is easy to blame everyone around, including ourselves for allowing them entry. In the end you are left with the folly of young men responding to the dares of equally foolish young girls. We never heard the final judgement, but discussed our security and continued to carry the men safely off the ships. It had actually, in our history, been an isolated incident.

Risley, some ten miles from Warrington, is a tough Remand Centre, which is rarely out of the news. The punishment would sometimes seem to be in advance of the verdict.

The Chaplain at Risley telephoned and asked me to visit two African seafarers, who were being held there before the hearing of their case. You see little of the place from the road, apart from the encircling wall with its rounded parapet and the large gates.

The welcome was formal, as I waited for two officers to accompany me into the Centre. They were big. They walked on either side of me and I began to feel guilty! It really was intimidating.

I was uncertain of the reason for my visit, but felt that it was not unreasonable for two seamen to ask to speak to a padre. The two gentlemen alongside me made it clear that they did not wish to talk to me and that I was wasting their time. My questions about Risley were pushed aside. I had hoped to meet the Chaplain, but he was not available.

I sat in a small room in front of a table. The walls were bare and apart from two chairs on the other side, there was no other furniture. My friends departed and I was told to wait. I sat for a long five minutes.

Then the two prisoners were brought in and we sat looking at each other. We were alone together.

They were African and in their early twenties. I explained who I was and gave them my card. I explained that I was there at the request of the Chaplain and in response to their desire to talk to the Missions to Seamen Chaplain. Words poured out of them and I had great difficulty in understanding. I urged them to be calm and speak slowly and separately.

It became clear that they wanted to speed up the legal process as they had already been in Risley for some months. They assumed that I had some influence.

I explained that I could not interfere with the law. They had legal aid and they should talk to the Risley Chaplain. I asked about their offence. They were very agitated and not explicit. As far as I could understand, it was a case of burglary and grievous bodily harm. I did not pursue the matter any further.

As simply as possible, I said that I would be pleased to contact the Missions to Seamen Chaplain in their home port, so that he might convey a message to their families.

There was an explosion of words. They quickly washed their hands of me and departed.

The walk back to the reception was again punctuated by remarks about time wasting. Mentally I agreed that I had achieved nothing, except a sad impression of Risley and a feeling of helplessness.

A few days later, I visited the Chief Constable of the Port Police, who was a good friend and a source of sound advice. I always felt at home there as I had "blessed the building" when it was first opened.

I explained my visit to Risley and complained about the over-long time that prisoners were on remand. I went into detail about what had happened. He was smiling. He asked me to repeat what I thought the charge was and I responded with "burglary with G.B.H".

It was some later that the whole sorry tale appeared in the press. I had been very innocent. A "girl", who was working the ships, had been savagely attacked by these men. She was still in hospital when I had called in Risley and the charge was serious.

Happy hour on Isle of Man
vessel along with Padre Ransom

I had misheard. The charge had been "buggery with grievous bodily harm". The two were found guilty and imprisoned.

One of the reasons for mentioning the Isle of Man, whilst thinking about the law, is that my old friend Norman Kelly was the Prison Chaplain there. He was also the Vicar of Castletown. Norman had come to the Mission in the 60's to work as a Lay Reader and, whilst with us, was ordained as Deacon and Priest. Naturally during my visits to the Island I would stay with him at the Vicarage. The crime level was very low, the birch was still in use and Norman was not over-stretched as the prison padre.

The Mission had a long contact with the Isle of Man and I had many friends there. Any padre worth the name would quickly uncover the fact that a visit to Liverpool's landing stage just before 10.30 any morning was essential to a life style. Each day, just before sailing, the Master served tea with slivers of hot buttered toast. The stage-master and I were frequent visitors, often only barely leaving the ship before she sailed. This was a great way to make friends. In later years, when I have listened to the Manx Seafarers' Choir, I can still savour the toast.

I first came across Bull's Blood at a wine tasting in Ramsey, where I had been asked to make a passionate speech on behalf of King George's Fund for Sailors. I was staying with Captain Westby Kissack and his wife Phyllis in Douglas. Westby gave me his brand new car for the evening. It was a great evening, I did my best and much monies were produced for the Fund. On the way home just before midnight, it all went wrong.

As I was motoring downhill into Laxey, the car stopped, the ignition was dead and the battery flat. So was Laxey! At midnight all the street lights are put out. It was pitch black, very cold, and Laxey had gone to bed.

In the darkness I found a telephone and explained my dilemma to Westby, who had been safely tucked up in bed.

"Stay where you are, Bob."

There seemed to be little choice.

"I'll use Phyllis's car. Stay in the phone box."

So I waited. I shivered in that box for one hour. There was no answer on Westby's phone. At last, at two o'clock the telephone rang in the box. It was the operator.

"Are you the gentleman who has broken down?"

I agreed that I certainly was.

"Stay where you are. The Captain will come to collect you. I've been calling every telephone kiosk on the Island. The Captain had gone back to sleep and then couldn't remember where you were."

There were many unanswered questions. At last I was rescued and I have never touched Bull's Blood since.

There was no greater challenge than the Annual Seafarers' Service in the Methodist Chapel at Port Erin. Every seat was taken and behind the preacher sat the Seamen's Choir. Never was the Manx Fishermen's Hymn better sung. I was given firm starting orders.

"Make it forty minutes and let it rip!"

I did my best.

Afterwards we all ended up in the home of Captain Griffin. Each person brought food and a chair. The house was full, every room and the stairs were occupied. The lady on the piano had badly arthritic hands, but she made the music dance. There were Manx poems and Manx stories and we all sang. I rendered the Welsh National Anthem and recited the Lord's Prayer in Welsh ... that was my full repertoire! It was the pre-Max Boyce era. They would have loved "Hymns and Arias". At half time, I telephoned D'rene in Liverpool.

"It sounds as though you are in a pub!"

Sadly I expect television has stopped such parties.

My final Service in the Island was in St. Mary in the Harbour in Castletown. The previous day, I had taken the address at the Blessing of the Harbour. A full gale had been blowing. It was so rough that no craft could have come near the harbour entrance. The local Prize Silver Band blew heartily and we all did our best. I received no complaints ... not a word could be heard above the wind!

That Sunday night in St. Mary in the Harbour, after yet another forty minutes in the pulpit, we had tea and cakes in the pews. Then we went at it again. It was "Any Requests" for almost two hours. Then I realised that, in the Isle of Man, no-one rushes home for Bergerac or Esther Rantzen on the box.

The normal crossing to the Isle of Man took four hours. There was one Monday, when I faced the return trip, and the wind was again at full blast and the Captain's wife had sent a couple of tablets to help my crossing to Liverpool. I had never been sea-sick, but she was a formidable lady, so I obeyed. I had been given a day cabin, so I retired there for a quiet read.

Apparently, the steward failed to arouse me for my elevenses. It was a tough crossing. The journey actually took six hours. I missed it! I was shaken awake at the Liverpool stage, a car was sent for and I was taken home to bed. No-one had mentioned that I had taken two of Phyllis Kissacks' rock-blasting, superior strength, sleeping tablets.

The real reason for putting the Isle of Man into a chapter on "the law" was because I can never remember ever seeing a policeman over there. It must be beyond the arm of the law.

23.

The Tall Ships

Whenever I am asked to recall the most memorable event in my Liverpool years, I have not the slightest hesitation.

"Let's talk about the five magic days at the back end of July in 1984, when every day was like Christmas Day."

Those of us who shared the experience will have no question about the wonder of it all. Those were the days when the Tall Ships came up the Mersey. I remember it well... I was there!

You cannot feel the same about a river after you have glimpsed a sailing ship quietly edging her way out of a dawn mist, when you happen to glance the top-mast before the rest of her beauty emerges. The fact that she happened to be on her auxiliary motor is forgotten in the glory of it all.

The Sail Training Association had organised two races. One followed the route taken by Jacques Cartier from St. Malo to Quebec in 1534. There were stop-overs for the crew at Bermuda, Halifax and Gaspe on the way out. Then the return journey was across the North Atlantic from Sydney in Nova Scotia to Merseyside. That was some race.

The second race was the Cutty Sark Tall Ships "little" race from Frederickshaven in Denmark, through the Fair Isle Sound to Greenock and then on to Merseyside to join the trans-Atlantic fleet. It was also an exciting and memorable voyage.

Liverpool was riding high. The International Garden Festival was proving to be an all-time winner for the four million people who came from all over the world. In the Mission we spent the summer taking crews almost every day to that Festival. It was a winner. Our football teams had won everything on offer in the English competitions, as well as the European Cup. We were the greatest. Liverpool was ready for the Tall Ships.

They came from many ports and nations. A large number of the ships sat just across the road from the Mission in Albert Dock. Pride of interest for many were the Swedish ships, the Falken and the Gladan. They happened to be "manned" by girls.

The City was to produce a video on the Tall Ships and I chanced to be going up the gangway of one of those Swedish ships at the right moment. I lost count of the number of times I went up that gangway before the camera team was satisfied. I think the technicians were concentrating on other matters. Those young ladies were the centre of attention throughout the stay. There was no language barrier.

Over in Vittoria Dock in Birkenhead in the cool of evening, we watched as the German three-masted barque, Gorch Fock, slowly came into the system. Aboard wer 69 permanent crew and 200 cadets. Those young lads, in orange jackets, dressed the yard-arms with a blaze of colour. We clapped and cheered our welcome. And, then, a German lad, surely the brightest of the bright, on top of the topmost mast stuck his fist in the air and shouted, "Oggy! Oggy! Oggy!" There was a moment of complete silence, as his voice echoed around the sheds and, as one, some two thousand folk in Birkenhead responded. The roar must have convinced the people in Wirral that the "Welsh are coming!"

As each vessel berthed, the crews quickly scattered among the fleet. Clambering down a quayside ladder, I joined the group on the deck of Dark Horse; she was very small. There I found liquorice allsorts of languages and nations. The Captain called for coffee. The "Aye, Aye" was the response from the galley down below. Soon ten mugs of brew arrived served by a Russian boy, who had been adopted by the rest of the crew. I believe he spent most of his time aboard.

And, then, there was music. Everyone sung their own shanties and songs and they all learned each other's favourites and shared the joy of togetherness. There were guitars and whistles and pipes and squeeze boxes and there was only the one language of music.

Yet another coffee was drunk aboard the Sea Cadet Association's Royalist, and another improbable tale was told. The story went that their Lordship's up in London had sent a message.

"Royalist, where are you?"

There had been a problem and lack of wind had put them out of schedule. There had been no time to sail around the top of Scotland. The response to the call was succinct.

"Royalist, latitude this and longitude that and altitude as follows."

They were quickly asked, "Repeat same." They did. Royalist happened to be in the middle of the Caledonian Canal and the altitude above sea level was correct! It was a good story well matched by the coffee.

The Mission's formal contribution was to organise the Service of Thanksgiving in Liverpool Parish Church at Pier Head. It had to be in many languages. The lessons were read in six, the prayers in two and each hymn had eight translations. The Liverpool University Staff were tremendous in their support and vied with each other to take part. We assembled as many clergy as possible from seafaring sources, together with our Bishop and the Archbishop. The Service flowed along, helped by Tony Davies and some of the Spinners singing their Liverpool songs and shanties. We made the rafters ring. All was well. I had spent days aboard the ships to ensure that each one was represented and knew that we were a family "at prayer." I trust each person felt the same emotion as I did when we all recited the Lord's Prayer in our own tongue.

We are rightly proud of our Town Hall in Liverpool and it was a special occasion when the City Fathers invited each ship to be represented at a formal dinner. It was a splendid affair. We ate long and well and wined at our ease, as the tales were told yet again.

There was a short speech of welcome from the Lord Mayor and the response was given by the Captain of the Sagres. He stood over six feet tall, straight backed, head well back to show his full set of whiskers. You could almost smell the sea. He boasted that he had written a superb speech and how lucky we were to hear him, but sadly it was in Portuguese and he thought that even the wine would not help us to understand.

"I will speak from the heart!"

It was an inspiration. He talked of the sea in all her moods. He told of the seafarer "with one hand for the ship, another for himself and another for his shipmate." We all understood what he meant. He spoke of the presence of God and of the Brotherhood of the Sea. I wish that I could have recorded that speech, because here was a seafarer communicating in the language of the sea.

And, then, we sang. One crew struck up, "We'll be sailing, Lord. Kumbya." The lights in the high chandeliers were dimmed, as we took up the refrain. Crew by crew, they led us in song. "Send us wind, Lord. Kumbya." For some twenty minutes we sang and, at the end, came the final chorus, "Kumbya here, Lord. Kumbya." And as far as I was concerned, the Lord had "come by here." It was a deeply spiritual moment shared by the very people, who were the Brotherhood of Man and the "family of seafarers," The singing had become a prayer.

You could not miss the Gloria. She was owned by the Colombian Navy and was the second youngest of all the square rigged sail training ships. She carried 60 cadets and was a four-masted barque, built in 1930. My visit to her in Vittoria Dock had its moments.

Hundreds of enthusiasts were queuing to climb the gangway to board this magnificent ship. Much in evidence were the young cadets, smartly dressed, and obviously very interested in the young ladies on the quayside.

I was welcomed aboard with much saluting and pipe blowing. In the Master's cabin were a number of people, sitting around the dining table. I was introduced by the Captain to a very striking lady, the Consul for Columbia on Merseyside. She had an equally beautiful name, Gloria Escobar.

Opening my briefcase, I explained the purpose of my visit, asking that the Captain and some crew members would attend the Thanksgiving Service. This did not take long and everyone relaxed. Coffee and sherry were produced and the Columbian Consul turned to me with a lovely smile and the words, "Well, boyo, and what part of Wales are you from?" Her Welsh accent was perfect and the explanation was simple. She was married to an engineer from Swansea, who worked in Columbia and just happened to be called Evans! No wonder I remember the Gloria with some affection!

The final event was the assembling of all the ship's companies at Pier Head and, headed by the Merseysippi Jazz Band, they marched through the City. The City stopped to applaud. As they marched, the crews intermingled, singing their way through the streets to the warmest Scouse welcome of the visit. Up the hill they strode to the Philharmonic Hall for the presentations. The Russians almost swept the board, but it did not matter. Everyone had won. Some were thankful just to arrive.

A Polish vessel had sailed into Vittoria Dock and they were in deep trouble. They had no food and no money. Quickly the word went out around the fleet and, with no embarrassment, help was given. It was more blessed to give than receive. There was happiness in sharing.

During the stay, Pier Head was alive with people, who came from many miles outside Liverpool to join in the Mersey welcome. The Mission was ideally placed to be a social centre. Like the Windmill Theatre, we never closed for five days. It was remarkable to stand outside Kingston House to look across at the ships and the thousands of folk, way after midnight, all smiling and talking to each other. It really did feel like five days of Christmas, when we all belonged to each other.

The final day came and for the first time the weather had failed us. There was one alarm. The Birkenhead police had found a wandering German seafarer, lost and bewildered. They asked for our help. Merseyside traffic was almost solid, but the Mission van won through, collected the stray and the lad jumped aboard, as the ship was clearing the last gate.

Both sides of the river were packed with people, but we had pulled rank and had a great vantage point. All our family and friends assembled at the Langton Gate entrance, opposite New Brighton, and we arrived there just as Britannia emerged out of the mid-day gloom to take up station for the farewell "Bon voyage!"

One by one, the "little ships" and the Tall Ships came down river to Britannia. As they turned to one side to pass in salute, each ship seemed to dip her prow in Royal obeisance. Every moment was a proud moment. Some of the vessels boasted guns and fired salvos to the joy of hundreds of thousands of cheering folk along the river bank. Many of those were not to leave Liverpool until the early hours of the next morning, Merseyside had stopped, too many cars, not enough roads. Many crews dressed the yardarms and made a brave and colourful picture. So they passed by and slipped into the afternoon mist.

Those ships took with them five glorious days and the hearts of every person on Merseyside. It was as though Christmas had come early that year.

24.

Ancient and Modern

A pre-war Royal Navy cruiser was docking in Seattle. A voice called out from the wharf.

"Are there any Scousers aboard?"

There was an immediate response from the ship.

"How do you think we got here!"

The sea is deep in the lives of Merseysiders. I was privileged to meet so many men, most on the verge of retirement and possibly the last to spend a lifetime at sea.

They were a generation to respect. I never cease to wonder at the courage of men brought ashore after surviving a torpedo hit on a tanker and then signing on for yet another trip on tankers.

Most of the care of the retired seamen undertaken by the Mission was the result of the dedication of Dolly Chandler. To all of us she was always, "Miss Chandler".

It all started in 1932, when the Ancient Mariners Club was created for men aged sixty-five with more than twenty years sea service. Thanks to Miss Chandler and Canon Bill Evans, when Kingston House was built in 1956, a new club room was allocated for these veterans.

When I came in 1961, that Club was flourishing. Any weekday morning, there would be some twenty men. If you lived alone in a bed-sit in the back streets somewhere, it was good to meet friends and be warm. The large teapot was never empty. Each morning they played "penny bingo" ... I was taught how to call! Then they would stroll around Pier Head and tell their tales. We held good old-fashioned Smoking Concerts with hot-pot and apple pie. The entertainment was all home made. Songs were sung, poems were recited and nothing was expurgated. We even had our own expert on the spoons. Happily I was too young to participate. Most of us smoked our pipes and my pouch took a hammering!

At Christmas over two hundred sat down for a turkey dinner and the pud and mince pies and crackers and carols. We wore our funny hats and some just went to sleep. Amongst the men were ten retired stewardesses and of them, Lily Wilkinson, took over the work of Dolly Chandler, when she died.

Christmas in Kingston House
for the Ancient Mariners Club

In the summer, we had two coach trips, taking our own food and receiving marvellous hospitality from Mothers' Unions and Ladies Guilds wherever we went. They provided even more food and the occasional crate of ale. Those crates and the statutory "pub halt" made the return journey a series of stops in the Cheshire lanes.

Eventually, the numbers dwindled and when we moved to Colonsay House, the Ancient Mariners Club was ended. We changed our approach when we became the agents for the Shipwrecked Mariners' Society. We doubled the recipients of grants in five years, and it meant that we visited the men in their homes; this was more effective and of greater value to them. That work will go from strength to strength.

Ships have changed dramatically since my early days. One large vessel can arrive in Royal Seaforth at eight in the evening and twelve hours later she will have sailed. There will be no more than eighteen men aboard with no time to get ashore. That ship would equal the carrying capacity of possibly ten ships in the 50's an 60's, each of which might have as many as 100 crew, and those ten vessels might stay in dock for three weeks. No wonder our docks looked busy!

Moving to Colonsay House put us nearer to the working dock system and enabled us to collect men off their ships, if only for a two hour break. Most modern seafarers are from the Third World. Many sign on for at least a year and are very poorly paid. Our response is to give them a warm welcome, which will not grab any headlines, but this is our work.

"Lord, when was it that we saw you hungry and fed you, or thirsty and gave you drink, a stranger and took you home, or naked and clothed you? When did we see you ill or in prison, and come to visit you? And the king will answer, "I tell you this; anything you did for one of my brothers here, however humble, you did for me."

Matthew 25. vv 37-40.

Our work should be judged on those words, which are as relevant today, as they have been for the last two thousand years.

What is happening in the Mission tonight? In the lounge there will be groups of men chatting in various languages. Some buy a drink ... a lager, a non-alcoholic beer, tea, coffee, coke. Foreign currency is being changed at the correct rate. Two men are

Colonsay House

oblivious to all around as they forget about time over a chess board. There are postcards to buy and leave for us to post. The bookcase is full of help-yourself paper backs. A peep into the Chapel ... just a moment for the family. A game of pool is under way. The first of the two videos are starting ... relax in an armchair with Clint Eastwood. A game of darts is played in the far corner. Time to call the folks at home. The Mission staff will sort out the international exchange and the payment in any currency. All too soon the evening has gone and the Mission mini-bus is waiting to return to the ship.

The Mission will always need money. Much help for capital expenditure comes from various sources. The need has to be proved. King George's Fund for Seafarers, the Merchant Navy Welfare Board, the Marine Society, the Liverpool Sailors Home Trust, the Philip Holt Trust, the Inverclyde Bequest, the Skelton Bounty, all have helped in the past. Above all monies came from our many friends on Merseyside, the little people who believe in the value of the work.

People shake their heads and say, "It's all over. It will never be the same again. The Port is dead." And I know that they are wrong.   It is not easy to digest the facts about the Port when minds have closed and the funeral rites have been read.   Just a few facts might help.

When I retired in 1989, the Port handled 20.3 million tons of cargo.   In 1994, the figure is 30.7 (includes the Medway ports of Sheerness and Chatham which are now owned and operated by the M.D.H.C.)   29.3 millions were handled in Liverpool.

Padre John Simmons continues the care for all
travel on the highway of the seas

Each year the Royal Seaforth Container Terminal has attracted more trade, e.g., 12 new contracts in the last 4 years.   There is a weekly service to Montreal, trading with Australia, New Zealand, the Eastern Seaboard of North America, sailings to the Mediterranean, Europe, Scandinavia, the Baltic and Ireland, forest trade from South Africa, Eastern Canada and Brazil. Another weekly service goes to Spain, then others to Portugal and Latvia.   A daily roll-on and roll-of and lift-on and lift-off cares for Belfast and Dublin.   The Port of Liverpool Euro Rail Terminal serves Europe via the Channel Tunnel with daily services to Italy, Spain, Switzerland, Germany, France and

Luxembourg. Liverpool to Paris in 15 hours, Milan in 36 hours, both indicate the speed at which freight can be moved into Europe.

In the so-called "heyday" of the 50's and 60's as many as 14,000 dockers were employed. Today 600 discharge and load similar volumes of cargo. Liverpool imports more grain than any other U.K. port, exports over a million tons of scrap metal each year and is a major port for timber and edible oils and fats.

Large container ships turn around in twelve hours. Haulage trucks deliver and collect containers in just forty minutes. Bulk carriers are discharged at the Royal Seaforth Grain Terminal at the rate of 20,000 tons a day, enabling the massive Panama sized vessels to be unloaded in three and a half days.

The Liverpool and Birkenhead Freeport serves over 80 countries with five million pounds worth of goods a week. It is big business.

The modern Port of Liverpool is here to stay. It is a gateway into the world and the Mersey Mission to Seamen will continue its care for all who travel on the highway of the seas.